Intelligent Business
Workbook

Upper Intermediate
Business English

| Louise Pile |

Pearson Education Limited
Edinburgh Gate
Harlow
Essex CM20 2JE
England
and Associated Companies throughout the world.

www.intelligent-business.org

First published 2006
Second impression 2007

Intelligent Business Upper Intermediate Workbook for pack
ISBN: 978-0-582-84685-2

Intelligent Business Upper Intermediate Workbook Audio CD
for pack
ISBN: 978-0-582-84059-1

Intelligent Business Upper Intermediate Workbook and CD
pack
ISBN: 978-0-582-84699-9

Set in Economist Roman 10.5 /12.5

Printed in Spain by Graficas Estella

Acknowledgements

The author would like to thank the editor, Gill Stacey.

The publishers are grateful to The Economist for permission
to adapt copyright material on page 5 (© 2005), pages 6 and 79
(© 2005), page 11 (© 2004), page 19 (© 2005), page 21 (© 2005),
page 26 (© 2004), page 30 (© 2005), page 31 (© 2004), pages 31
and 82 (© 2004), page 31 (© 2004), page 34 (© 2005), pages 35 and
82 (© 2004), page 38 (© 2004), page 43 (© 2004), pages 42 and 84
(© 2005), page 47 (© 2005), page 49 (© 2005), pages 50 and 85
(© 2005), page 51 (© 2005), page 55 (© 2005), pages 58 and 86
(© 2004), page 59 (© 2005), pages 62 and 87 (© 2005), page 67
(© 2005), page 68 (© 2005), page 70 (© 2004), page 72 (© 2004),
pages 75 and 87 (© 2004). All articles copyright of The
Economist Newspaper Limited. All rights reserved.

We are also grateful to the following for permission to
reproduce copyright material:
News International Syndication for an extract from "The secret
of teamwork" by Des Dearlove published in *The Times* 8th
August 2002; Let's Talk Business Today Magazine for extracts
from "My best and worst Business Decision: Steve Walker" and
Taking the hassle out of finance: Oakwood Financial
Management – the complete solution" published in *Let's Talk
Business Today* Volume 3, Issue 3, April 2005; and Haymarket
Business Publications Limited for extracts from "Ride the early
Wave" by Drew Barrand published in *PR Week* 6th May 2005
and "Littlewoods rethinks catalogue strategy" by Ian Hill
published in *PR Week* 6th May 2005.
In some instances we have been unable to trace the owners of
copyright material and we would appreciate any information
that would enable us to do so.

Photograph acknowledgements
Alamy/Profimedia.CZ.s.r.o. 29; Aston Martin 32; BAA Aviation
Photo Library/Andy Wilson 8, /Simon Kreitem 10;
Corbis/Reuters 1r, 3b, 24t, 36, /Yang Liu 7, /Steve Chenn 23. /
Sygma/Susana Raab 28, /FK Photo 38, /Images.com 40, /Patrik
Giardino 56; Empics/AP/Ben Margot 48, /Paul Sakuma 51; Getty
Images/ Chad Slattery 11, /Steve Bly 13, /David Buffington 20,
/Greg Ceo 21, /Frederic Lucano 25, /Jonathan Kirn 53, /Billy
Hustace 58; Honda 1c; Kos Picture Source 12; Nokia 62; Panos
Pictures/Mikkei Ostergaard 52; Pearson Education Limited,
Managers Not MBAs by Henry Mintzberg 59; Rex Features/Paul
Cooper 33; Still Pictures/Hartmut Schwarzbach 1l;
Topham/Image Works 24b, /National Pictures 34, /Hubert Reece
41, /Matt Miller 43.

The cover photographs have been kindly supplied by Still
Pictures (left), Honda (centre) and Corbis (right).

Picture Researcher: Liz Moore

Illustrated by Kathy Baxendale, John Bradley and Phil Garner
(Beehive)

Designed by Cathy May/Endangered Species

Contents

Technology

A more accessible internet

Broadband is dramatically changing the way we use the internet. Now, wireless internet access is playing an increasing role in the way we use computers. Wi-Fi technology allows us to surf the net without wires through a small base station. What sort of developments might we see in the future, and how soon will they arrive? **Page 21.**

Energy

Sustainable design and technology

The efficient use and production of energy is more important today than ever before. Large buildings such as office blocks take a lot of energy to run, but much is wasted through inefficient design. The proponents of 'green architecture' aim to reduce energy consumption and its environmental impact, while creating a more pleasant working environment. What other benefits can it have? **Page 43.**

Unit 1 Alliances

Vocabulary:	**Alliances**
Language:	**Review of tenses**
Career skills:	**Building relationships**
Writing:	**Email agreeing to a meeting**

| Vocabulary

1 Use the clues to find the words in the puzzle.

1 goals
2 to weaken
3 a conflict
4 having business in many countries
5 bringing together
6 sensible, wise
7 takeover of another company
8 company with a diverse portfolio of businesses

1				T	A	R	G	E	T	S			
2				F	A	L	T	E	R				
3				C	L	A	S	H					
4			M	U	L	T	I	N	A	T	I	O	N A L
5	I	N	T	E	G	R	A	T	I	O	N		
6		P	R	U	D	E	N	T					
7				A	C	Q	U	I	S	I	T	I O N	
8	C	O	N	G	L	O	M	E	R	A T E			

2 Complete the sentences with *on, over, in, up, out* or *down.*

1 The company has seen an improvement ____*in*____ market share.
2 BusTec and SweFact have decided to co-operate _____ a major project.
3 It was a mistake to invest _____ Silco shares.
4 The CEO announced that the company would be taken _____ by Kids2grow.
5 I think we should concentrate _____ our core competences.
6 It's important that we don't give _____ control of the business.
7 The type of kitchen equipment Resolve produces is going _____ of fashion.
8 Can we really afford to turn _____ their offer?
9 Without new investment, the company is likely to go _____ of business.
10 The economy is slowing _____ – we can't afford to take risks right now.

3 Complete the table below.

	verb	noun
1	integrate	*integration*
2		bid
3	partner	
4		acquisition
5	consolidate	
6		achievement
7	merge	
8		success

Reading | **Read the article about drug firm takeovers. Then choose the best sentence below to fill each of the gaps.**

a   There are few synergies between the two sorts of drug manufacture.

b   Companies need to be big enough to dominate distribution channels to wholesalers.

c   Generic drug sales totalled $30 billion last year in the eight biggest markets.

d   But not everyone is happy.

e   The acquisition will make Sandoz the world's largest generic drugmaker.

The Economist

Business

Combination therapy

Novartis buys two generic drugmakers

Novartis, a Swiss drug giant, has announced its purchase of Hexal, a German generics firm, and a sister company in America, Eon Labs, for a combined cost of $8.3 billion.

Novartis already has a generic drug division, called Sandoz, which struggled last year to sell $3 billion-worth of drugs, roughly one-third more than Hexal and Eon Labs combined. ¹___e___ It will also give it a stronghold in Germany, the world's second-largest generics market. ²_____ They are likely to grow by a healthy 10% a year until 2009, says IMS Health, a data and consultancy firm, as public and private buyers in Europe and America look for ways to cut their drugs bill.

Only a few years ago big drug firms, which had bought generics companies in the hope of making easy money, were busy trying to off-load them. ³_____ Generic drug-making is "a gloves-off business compared to the gentlemanly boxing match which is Big Pharma," says Neal Hansen of Datamonitor, a research firm. In generics, success depends on being cheap enough to keep manufacturing and other costs down. ⁴_____ They also have to be fast enough to move in and out of markets as opportunity ebbs and flows. Staying ahead of the competition is a further challenge.

Novartis may make Sandoz big and broad enough to do that, at least for now. ⁵_____ Health activists, concerned about rising drug prices and restricted access to medicines, are already grumbling about the incursion of the big drug firms into the plucky underdog business of generics.

1 Before you listen to a business radio programme about Unilever, make notes on what you know about the company's area of business, its competitors and the problems it faces.

2 Now listen and complete the notes below.

Unilever

Unilever is an Anglo-Dutch (1) ... *multinational*

It is a large (2) *consumer goods* .... retailer.

Patrick Cescau is to become the company's (3) *chief executive*

Antony Burgmans will become the non-executive (4) ...... *chairman*

There are two possible (5) *takeover* ..... targets –

Colgate-Palmolive and Reckitt Benckiser.

Unilever's debts are (6) $ *15* b.

Last year sales fell by (7) ... *6* %

It has lowered its (8) ...... *performance* ... targets.

The company has some problems, for instance, not

enough (9) ...... *advertising* ....

3 Check that you understand the following words and phrases about mergers and acquisitions. Then listen again. Tick those used in the listening.

multinational   resources   stockmarket   rival   deal   partnership
competitiveness   profits   takeover targets   debts   integration
budget   market share   strategic   shareholder

1 Look at these sentences. Some are correct. Identify the correct sentences and find and correct the mistakes.

never borrow
1   We ~~are never borrowing~~ money at such high rates of interest.
2   He arrived late for the meeting because he had forgotten the time.
3   My colleague seems optimistic about the proposed takeover, although the company's shares have fallen.
4   The organisation certainly didn't expected as many culture clashes.
5   By the end of tomorrow we'll definitely *have* signed a deal.
6   The CEO's taking a back seat at the moment.
7   When ~~have you heard~~ *did you hear* from our rivals? Yesterday?
8   It *was* several weeks since I met our partners.
    has been

2 Read the conversation extracts and complete the gaps with phrases for building relationships.

1 A: I don't think _we've met_. I'm Sylvia Jacobs. We've spoken on the phone a few times.

B: Oh yes, of course. Hello!

2 A: _Here's my_ card.

B: Thank you. I'll definitely be in touch.

3 A: So, who do you work for?

B: Paul and Moger. We _offer electrical appliances and service_

4 A: Flately's is about to expand operations into China.

B: How interesting! I'd love _to hear more about it_

5 A: _When can we set up a_ meeting? Would Tuesday at 10 suit you?

B: That'd be just fine.

6 A: _What did you think of_ the main speaker?

B: I found him really inspiring, actually.

7 A: _How can I help_ you?

B: I'd like some information about your Scandinavian furniture, please.

Writing Read the email about a possible meeting. Write an email in reply:

– thanking Lesley for her email
– expressing interest in meeting
– saying what you would like to discuss
– giving a possible time and date to meet.

Then compare your answer with the suggested answer on page 90.

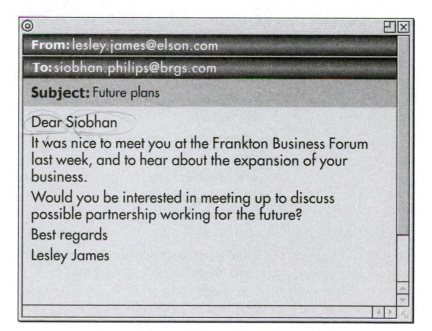

From: lesley.james@elson.com

To: siobhan.philips@brgs.com

Subject: Future plans

Dear Siobhan

It was nice to meet you at the Frankton Business Forum last week, and to hear about the expansion of your business.

Would you be interested in meeting up to discuss possible partnership working for the future?

Best regards

Lesley James

Unit 2 Projects

Unit 2
Projects

Mission to accomplish

Vocabulary:	**Projects**
Grammar:	**Articles**
Career skills:	**Setting goals**
Writing:	**Cover letter for a job application**

Vocabulary

1 Match each of the following nouns with one set of verbs.

a project   a problem   a solution   resources   a plan   equipment

1	complete deliver run manage	_a project_	4	find implement propose adopt	_____
2	estimate control allocate identify	_____	5	test deliver purchase install	_____
3	deal with tackle handle solve	_____	6	prepare come up with put together carry out	_____

2 Complete the sentences with the correct options a–c.

1 The CEO has decided to _____c_____ production of the XR20 model to India.

   a initiate   b executive   c outsource

2 We're hoping to be _____ a multi-million-pound contract shortly.

   a selected   b awarded   c obtained

3 Please could you fax me the agreed technical _____ for the Salford Cycle model.

   a specification   b standardisation   c subcontractor

4 The project has overrun and we've therefore had to _____ up the costs.

   a spin   b bump   c cater

5 We need to decide when to bring Jenny in on the project. Perhaps at the planning _____ ?

   a stage   b schedule   c status

3 Complete the table below.

	verb	noun
1	construct	*construction*
2		production
3	supply	
4	install	
5		review
6		allocation

Language check **1** Complete the email with *a/an*, *the* or no article at all.

From: atul.menyani@beestons.com

To: mandy.ellis@beestons.com

Subject: Next week

Atul

Thanks for agreeing to look after my project while I am on ¹ _(no article)_ holiday next week. As I said when we spoke ² _____ last week, the project really needs to be launched by ³ _____ end of June at ⁴ _____ latest. It currently looks as if we should complete all the work on time and within ⁵ _____ budget, so you shouldn't have too many problems while I'm in ⁶ _____ Netherlands. If you do need ⁷ _____ help though, just give Carl a call on 039 48395. He's ⁸ _____ main engineer on the project and has been working on it from ⁹ _____ start – if anyone will know what to do, it'll be him!

There are ¹⁰ _____ few things you could do for me, if you don't mind. Firstly, would you mind sending ¹¹ _____ email to Frank Smith (his details are on my desk) to see how ¹² _____ marketing team are getting on with our publicity leaflets, etc. Also, there's ¹³ _____ report on my desk which needs to be copied and given to Maxine, ¹⁴ _____ Production Director's PA. Do you think you could also write ¹⁵ _____ letter to ¹⁶ _____ company organising the PR for ¹⁷ _____ project, asking for ¹⁸ _____ copies of all the press releases they have sent out.

Finally, I'm expecting ¹⁹ _____ supplier from ²⁰ _____ CTR Communications to phone to arrange ²¹ _____ meeting. I think the 22nd will be ²² _____ best day for me. If he can manage that too, could you book ²³ _____ boardroom for us?

Thanks again for all your help.

Mandy

2 Put the words in the correct order to make useful phrases for setting goals.

1 the / what / project / schedule / the / is / for?
What is the schedule for the project?

2 do / need / to / when / I / the / get / information / you / to?

3 think / do / July / is / feasible / you?

4 the / of / in / you / need / will / way / what / resources?

5 we / should / think / aim / I / to / complete / work / Tuesday / by / the.

6 reasonable / that / does / sound / you / to?

7 exactly / what / is / involved?

8 much / you / for / how / are / budgeting?

Listening 2 ⊙ T3

1 Listen to two colleagues discussing a project and answer the questions.

1 What are the project team developing?
A new office workstation that staff control from the touch of a button.

2 What advantages will the new workstation have?

3 When will it be launched?

4 When will the press release be sent to the media?

2 Listen again. What phrases for setting goals used in Language Check 2 do the speakers use?

3 Read the audioscript on page 79 and check your answers.

Writing You see the job advertisement below in a national newspaper and decide to apply for it. Write a cover letter to send with your CV.

Then compare your answer with the suggested answer on page 90.

PROJECT MANAGER

- Are you good at problem-solving?

- Do you have experience of completing complex projects to time and within budget?

Build-2-Go is a well-respected construction company with 750 staff throughout the country. We are currently looking for a well-organised and dynamic project manager to be based in our Luton office. The successful candidate will have experience in managing people and resources, and good communication skills.

For a full job description, visit www.B2G.com
To apply, send your CV and cover letter to Myra.Watson@B2G.com

1 Complete the article about software projects with the following words.

negligence   glitch   system   programs   budget
delays   launch   plan   schedule

2 Read the article again. Are the statements *true* or *false*?

1   There were five serious air crashes in September.   *false*

2   The air-traffic control system had problems with their computer program.

3   A report suggested that the majority of software projects take longer than expected.

4   The writer blames computer programmers and their managers for projects failing.

5   Longhorn is an example of a project that went according to plan.

The Economist

Business

Managing complexity

Software projects fail to deliver

On September 14th, the radios in an air-traffic control centre in Palmdale, California shut down, grounding hundreds of flights in southern California and Nevada, and leading to five mid-air encounters between aircraft unable to talk to the ground controllers. Disaster was averted because aircraft managed to communicate with more distant back-up facilities. But why did Palmdale's radios fail?

A ¹ *glitch* in the software running the system meant the computers had to be re-booted every 30 days, and somebody forgot to do so. But software running a mission-critical ² _____ should not have to be restarted every month. The culprit: poor design and no contingency ³ _____ .

As software has become more and more pervasive in business and government, and more complicated, the impact of poor software design has been steadily growing. A study earlier this year by the Standish Group, a technology consultancy, estimated that 30% of all software projects are cancelled, nearly half come in over ⁴ _____ , 60% are considered failures by the organisations that initiated them, and nine out of ten come in late.

A 2002 study by America's National Institute of Standards (NIST), a government research body, found that software errors cost the American economy $59.5 billion annually. Worldwide, it would be safe to multiply this figure by a factor of two. So who is to blame for such ⁵ _____ ?

Delays are common in numerous industries – few large infrastructure projects, for instance, are completed either on time or within budget. But it is peculiar to software that billions of dollars and other resources can be used only for nothing useful to result.

At a very basic level, it is the fault of the software engineers who are writing the ⁶ _____ , and of their bosses. Even companies that specialise in software development suffer from ⁷ _____ and being behind ⁸ _____ . An obvious example is Microsoft: its "Longhorn", the long-heralded successor to its Windows XP operating system, was originally scheduled for ⁹ _____ this year. Longhorn is now not expected before mid-2006, and many of its key features have been put off until 2007.

Unit 3 Teamworking

Vocabulary: **Teamworking**
Language: **Modal forms**
Career skills: **Team building**
Writing: **Email requesting information**

The stuff teams are made of

| Vocabulary

1 Complete the tips for effective meetings with the following verbs.

monitor   ensure   involve   establish   choose
keep   assign   create   plan   ask

Tips for effective meetings

1 _Choose_ a suitable location for the meeting.
2 _plan_ the agenda carefully.
3 _establish_ clear ground rules.
4 _create_ a relaxed, open atmosphere.
5 _monitor_ progress regularly during the meeting.
6 _keep_ everyone focused.
7 _ask_ someone to take the minutes.
8 _ensure_ there are plenty of breaks.
9 _involve_ all relevant staff in the decision-making process.
10 _assign_ clear tasks for people at the end.

2 Which word is the odd one out in each set?

	a		b		c		d	
1	a	achieve	b	accomplish	c	reach	d	fail
2	a	proposal	b	aim	c	target	d	objective
3	a	pessimism	b	criticism	c	scepticism	d	enthusiasm
4	a	efficient	b	concise	c	precise	d	tedious
5	a	co-operate	b	collaborate	c	collate	d	communicate
6	a	chairperson	b	facilitator	c	mission	d	participant

3 How many nouns related to teams can you find in the word search?

b	m	e	e	t	i	n	g
u	b	s	p	i	r	i	t
i	c	k	i	a	g	w	m
l	f	c	d	j	i	o	e
d	l	e	a	d	e	r	m
i	m	e	p	s	h	k	b
n	n	m	o	r	a	l	e
g	o	p	l	a	y	e	r

Writing   **Read the advert and then write an email (60–80 words) to Simon at Take Part:**

– saying where and when you saw their advert
– requesting a brochure
– stating the activities you are particularly interested in.

Then compare your answer with the suggested answer on page 90.

Looking for team-building events with a difference?
Look no further!

TAKE PART can offer you and your colleagues a whole range of tailor-made sporting activities:

- windsurfing
- white-water rafting
- yachting
- bungee-jumping
- orienteering
- golfing … and many more!
- mountaineering
- cycling

Email Simon Hunt on take-part@deft.com for a brochure.
Don't forget to tell us where you saw this ad!

Rewrite the underlined phrases, keeping the same meaning. Use the modal verbs *might*, *can*, *must* and *should*.

You must

1 It's essential that you attend the meeting.
2 It's vital that team members work closely together. *You must*
3 It isn't a very good idea for you to always work through lunch. *You shouldn't*
4 No-one's turned up – I don't think Mark has reminded them about the meeting. *Mark might not have*
5 I recommend that you hold the meeting at the Imperial Hotel. *You should*
6 I'm not sure but I think I wrote up the minutes. *I might have written up*
7 I think Joe is caught in traffic – he often is. *Joe might be*
8 My advice to you is to cancel the team-building event. *You should*
9 It wasn't a good idea to get the boss involved. *You shouldn't have gotten*
10 I'm sure he isn't the person to blame – he wasn't even here! *He can't be*

---

1 **Read the article and answer the questions.**

1 What examples of team-building events are given?

sporting (e.g. rowing); problem-solving (e.g. crossing river)

2 Whose research has dominated theories of teamwork?
3 What did Henley College offer the researcher?
4 What did his tests reveal?

THE SECRET OF TEAMWORK

In offices around the world, there are pictures of rowing crews and tug-of-war teams exhorting employees to be "good team players". Managers are constantly reminded that the team is the thing.

The fortunate ones are sent to "bond" in team activities at secluded corporate retreats. The unlucky ones are dispatched on team-building sessions to the side of a mountain and asked to bridge rivers with little more than elastic bands and burgeoning team spirit.

But despite their enthusiasm for teams, until recently the way companies understood what made successful teamwork remained rooted in the 1960s. For 35 years, the ideas of Professor Meredith Belbin have ruled. Generations of managers have grown up with his theories.

Professor Belbin's theories date back to research in 1967, when an initiative at Henley Management College presented him with a rare opportunity to study teamwork in a controlled environment. Henley introduced a computer-based business game into one of its courses. The game pitted teams against each other, and offered Professor Belbin, then at the Industrial Training Research Unit at University College, London, his own laboratory of teamwork. It remains a benchmark study.

Team members conducted a series of personality and psychometric tests. From his observations, Professor Belbin discovered that certain combinations of personality types performed more successfully than others. He identified the nine archetypal roles required to make up an ideal team: the Plant – provides the team with imagination and ideas; the Co-ordinator – clarifies goals and promotes decision-making; the Shaper – is dynamic and finds ways around obstacles; the Teamworker – provides the social lubrication for the team, and so on.

2 **How many words can you find in the article that go after the word *team*? How many more can you think of?**

1 Put the sentences in the correct order to make a conversation between two colleagues. Then listen to check your answers.

a Well, OK. I'll get onto the hotel straight away. ☐

b So, Gina, how are things going? [1]

c Well, we wanted to book the Pesta Hotel for the conference ... ☐

d Not too good actually, Bill. ☐

e Go on, I'm listening. ☐

f Oh dear. Tell me more. ☐

g Well, the venue's free every weekend in June except for the 17th – which is when we need it. ☐

h That's a great idea, but it's so soon – and there's so much to organise. ☐

i Don't panic. Let's look at ways of getting round this problem. How about holding the conference on the 10th of June? ☐

j If anyone can do it, you can. And, of course, all the team will be here to help you. ☐

2 Now look at the audioscript on page 80 and underline positive phrases the speakers use.

Professor O'Driscoll gives a presentation at a business forum about team roles. Listen and choose the correct options a–c.

1 What did Belbin think about teams?   *a*

  a A team's success depends on its members carrying out their roles effectively.

  b Teams cannot be successful unless all individual members get on.

  c It is important for teams continually to review their effectiveness.

2 Belbin's approach helps people to

  a recognise each other's strengths and weaknesses.

  b understand how to develop individuals' skills.

  c see how the team is put together.

3 What did the speaker's research involve?

  a It compared a small number of sport and music teams.

  b It identified the most competent team members.

  c It focused on the skills all teams need to be effective.

4 The research revealed that

  a groups of musicians were the most stable teams.

  b teams were constructed differently and for different reasons.

  c the needs of teams changed over time.

5 The model the researchers developed

  a sets out the factors that promote team success.

  b shows the links between different teams.

  c divides teams into smaller units.

6 The model can help people to identify

  a potential managers within a team.

  b how to develop a team further.

  c the most appropriate activities for a team to carry out.

Unit 4 Information

The real-time economy

Vocabulary:	**Information**
Language:	**Question forms**
Career skills:	**Questioning techniques**
Writing:	**Short report interpreting information from a graph**

| Vocabulary

1 Match the pairs.

1	code	a	network
2	communications	b	espionage
3	wireless	c	technology
4	industrial	d	sensor
5	electronic	e	directory
6	staff	f	surveillance
7	classified	g	ads
8	information	h	of conduct

2 Complete the sentences with the correct options a–c.

1 We need to update the ___c___ on this machine, for instance, get the latest version of Word.

   a hardware   b program   c software

2 The new information tool will help us become more _____ and streamlined.

   a efficient   b verbose   c volatile

3 It's one thing gathering information. It's quite another to _____ it where you'll find it again easily.

   a process   b exchange   c store

4 I wasn't really concentrating – I went on to _____ .

   a auto-pilot   b real-time   c speed-up

5 We'll need to _____ the situation very carefully.

   a monitor   b present   c download

6 HR have set up a telephone _____ to deal with enquires.

   a intranet   b spreadsheet   c hotline

7 The new information management system has had a direct _____ on our financial situation.

   a impact   b response   c connection

8 You'll find all the files you need on the company _____ .

   a circuit-breaker   b application   c network

9 How would you judge our _____ in relation to our annual targets?

   a measurement   b performance   c goal

10 There are about 1,000 regular _____ of the new system.

   a officers   b users   c subsidiaries

3 Match the words and definitions.

> network   database   gather   hardware   intelligence
> procedure   software   spreadsheet   surveillance   data

1 organised set of information stored in a computer   *database*
2 collect information, ideas, etc.
3 computer machinery and equipment
4 information collected about the activities of an organisation or individual
5 set of computers connected to each other and operating as part of the same system
6 accepted method and order of doing something
7 set of programs put into a computer to perform particular tasks
8 computer program that shows rows of figures and performs calculations with them
9 act of monitoring a person or group of people
10 information or facts about a particular subject that someone has collected

---

Language check   **1** Put the words in the correct order to make questions.

1 who / you / were / if / me / would / invite / you?
   If you were me, who would you invite?
2 updating / about / the / how / website?
3 I / you / how / don't / realise / busy / am?
4 a / we / have / shall / meeting / intranet / about / the?
5 files / the / know / you / do / downloaded / who?
6 any / to / have / idea / do / you / system / the / how / install?
7 the / you / get / would / do / to / what / information?
8 about / you / the / me / why / tell / didn't / hardware / new?

2 Decide which of the questions in exercise 1 are:

a an invitation   *2, 4*
b hypothetical
c negative
d embedded

3 Complete the gaps appropriately.

1 You weren't late for the meeting, _were you_ ?
2 That problem will really delay the launch of the software, _____ ?
3 You _____ show me the new machinery, _____ ?
4 He didn't tell you about the surveillance operation, _____ ?
5 Getting the new equipment _____ mean redundancies in the long-term, won't it?
6 The managers won't be coming to the trials, _____ ?

1 Read this dialogue about a new information tool. Use these phrases to complete the gaps in the questions. Then listen to the dialogue and check your answers.

are the benefits to users	does it stand for	don't ... do you
will there be	does the tool work	

A: I've just been reading about a new research tool called Doris. You ¹___*don't*___ know who has designed it, ²___*do you*___?

B: Yes, it was GNN, in partnership with Information 360, the software producer.

A: I see. Doris is a strange name. What ³_____?

B: Direct, online, read-time information system.

A: I can see why it's been shortened! So, how ⁴_____?

B: Well, as far as I understand it, the tool will be installed onto the GNN's regional news delivery network.

A: What ⁵_____?

B: Well, users will be able to download a toolbar that automates how information is delivered from various departments. It can also help users to search hard drives to locate documents.

A: ⁶_____ many users?

B: Yes, about 90,000 people, I think.

2 How would you categorise each question (open/closed/tag)?

Writing

The graph below shows the use of email in a number of countries. Using the information in the graph, write a short report (120–140 words) on:

- what information is shown in the graph
- where email usage is the highest/lowest
- where email has increased revenue the most/least.

Then compare your answer with the suggested answer on page 91.

Time spent accessing/responding to emails
2004, hours per day

Country	%
Philippines	84
Hong Kong	48
India	80
United States	48
Australia	45
Singapore	42
Canada	42
Mexico	66
South Africa	41
Taiwan	49
Netherlands	36
New Zealand	54
Spain	64
Sweden	43
Britain	47
Germany	32
Ireland	56
Italy	31
Japan	20
France	13
Poland	40
Turkey	54
Greece	45
Russia	46

* Percentage of businesses surveyed who agree that email and the internet have helped increase revenue

Source: Grant Thornton International

Read the article below and choose the correct options a–d.

1 According to paragraph 1, Mr Scoble   c
   a recently changed his job.
   b writes computer programs.
   c has two different roles.
   d was previously a manager at Microsoft.

2 The author says that Mr Scoble used to
   a live in Japan.
   b provide IT help to customers.
   c prefer to write his reports by hand.
   d be interested in rapid promotion.

3 Which of these statements is true?
   a Mr Scoble is related to Lenn Pryor.
   b People like his truthfulness.
   c He doesn't have his own PC.
   d He works normal office hours.

4 The author says that
   a managers are discouraging staff from blogging.
   b Mr Scoble only ever praises Microsoft.
   c Mr Schwarz does not see the value of blogging.
   d rivals are now copying Mr Scoble.

The Economist

Face value

1 Mr Scoble is, first, a blogger – i.e. somebody who keeps an online journal (called a "web log" or "blog") to which he posts thoughts and web links several times a day. But Mr Scoble is also an employee of Microsoft, the world's largest software company. Those two roles are intertwined. It was his blogging prowess that led to his job, and much of the job consists of blogging.

2 Mr Scoble started blogging four years ago. At the time, he worked for NEC, a Japanese technology company, and was based in Silicon Valley. Mr Scoble's area of expertise was tablet pcs – laptop computers that allow users to handwrite their notes. Mr Scoble used his blog to converse with NEC's customers, giving and monitoring tech support and gathering feedback.

3 All with such disarming honesty that his blog became a must-read for gadget lovers. This caught the attention of Lenn Pryor, who hired him. Mr Scoble simply kept doing what he was good at – and getting a large number of hits. His blog, which he has kept outside of Microsoft's computers, is usually posted in the wee hours after midnight.

4 Mr Scoble is at his best when he opines ruthlessly on Microsoft's technology. When Google or Apple or anybody else makes a better product, he blogs it. "I've been pretty harsh on Microsoft over the years," he says. This gives him credibility, and thus power. If somebody somewhere takes a swipe at Microsoft that is unfair, Mr Scoble can cry foul and actually have his readers concede the point.

5 Inspired in part by Mr Scoble's success, executives at other companies are starting their own blogs. Most daringly, Jonathan Schwartz, number two at Sun Microsystems, a large computer-maker, has blogged his thoughts about possible mergers in his industry, and thrown punches at Hewlett-Packard, IBM and other rivals. Bruce Lowry, PR boss at Novell, another software firm, has also announced he wants to get his executives blogging.

Unit 5 Technology

Vocabulary: **Technology**
Language: **Relative clauses**
Career skills: **Briefing**
Writing: **Email recommending a product**

Vocabulary

1 **Which is the odd one out in each set?**

1	a network	b	innovation	c	creativity	d	initiative
2	a update	b	improve	c	develop	d	install
3	a keypad	b	handset	c	access	d	screen
4	a profit	b	revenue	c	virus	d	returns
5	a subscribe	b	upload	c	browse	d	download
6	a component	b	device	c	coverage	d	appliance
7	a energy-efficient	b	multi-media	c	high-performance	d low-cost

2 **Match the verbs and nouns.**

1 extend   a waste
2 detect   b a virus
3 access   c revenue
4 install   d coverage
5 upload   e potential
6 boost   f the internet
7 recycle   g a file
8 maximise   h machinery

Reading 1

1 **Read the article opposite about technology. Are these statements *true* or *false*?**

1 Wi-Fi has greater coverage than WiMax.   *false*
2 Claims about WiMax have been exaggerated.
3 WiMax products still need to be accredited.
4 The launch of WiMax products on to the market will be postponed.
5 Some think WiMax will be used mainly in urban areas.

2 **Now underline the correct relative pronouns in brackets.**

3 Look at the article again. Find words with similar meanings.

1 influence   *impact*
2 can be used together
3 initial design to test
4 browse
5 elements or parts of
6 appliances
7 radio
8 connection between computers, etc.

The Economist

Business

Wireless internet

World domination postponed

TO HEAR some of its more enthusiastic supporters you might conclude that WiMax, [1] *which / who* is an emerging wireless-broadband technology, was about to take over the world. WiMax is similar to a long-range version of the popular Wi-Fi technology [2] *that / what* allows computers close to a small base-station to surf the internet without wires. Whereas Wi-Fi's range is limited to a few tens of metres, WiMax can, in theory, work over tens of kilometres, [3] *which / that* allows huge areas to be blanketed with wireless coverage. Hence the claims that WiMax will bring internet access to the five billion people [4] *who / what* currently lack it, or that it will render expensive "third-generation" (3G) mobile networks redundant.

The reality, however, is that WiMax has been hugely overhyped. Despite claims by several firms that they are offering WiMax technology today, the actual number of WiMax devices on the market is precisely zero. That is because the WiMax Forum, [5] *that / which* is a standards body that oversees the technology and ensures that components from different vendors work together, has yet to certify any devices with the WiMax label.

On January 24th it announced that pre-certification testing will begin in July, [6] *which / that* means that the first WiMax devices will be available only at the end of the year, six months later than expected. So far, equipment-makers can offer only "pre-WiMax" or "WiMax-ready" equipment, [7] *which / what* will, they promise, be compatible with WiMax devices when they appear.

The hype about its potential impact is now giving way to much scepticism about the technology's prospects. "I don't think it's completely hot air, but it won't live up to the early promise of the prototypes," says Jagdish Rebello of iSuppli, a market-research firm. WiMax, he says, will chiefly be used by telecoms firms in rural areas, to plug holes in their broadband coverage.

In some lines there is an extra word. Underline the incorrect word or write CORRECT next to the line number.

Breakthrough

CORRECT	0	A new gadget has recently come on the market,
	1	designed to encourage children to take the part in
	2	physical activity, rather than of watch TV. The tracking
	3	device is small enough and to fit into the youngest
	4	child's shoes, and works by counting the number of
	5	steps the child takes in. It transmits data through a
	6	radio signal to a base unit that plugged into the family's
	7	TV set. This unit it converts the child's steps into
	8	minutes – a hundred steps equals one minute of TV viewing
	9	time, so twelve thousand steps would be allow a child
	10	to watch two hours of TV. When the units seem run out,
	11	the TV signal is blocked, and can only be reactivated by the
		child taking more steps.

Writing **You are an assistant buyer for an electronics retailer. Write an email (60–80 words) to your boss, recommending that your outlet stocks one of the products below and giving your reasons why.**

Then compare your answer with the suggested answer on page 91.

	XBox360	Playstation 3
Brand:	Microsoft	Sony
Speed:	5 times more powerful than a home computer	10 times more powerful than a home computer
Memory:	512 MB	256 MB
Extras:	Wireless internet and controllers, DVD player	Wireless internet and controllers, DVD player
Cost:	£180 (expected)	£200 (expected)
Due:	in shops by November	in shops by next spring

Match the sentence halves.

1 These briefings will focus on   *b*
2 As this chart shows
3 Probably the best way to do this
4 Martin, can you make
5 I want the PR team to
6 To get results,

a the project is running two months behind schedule.
b updating the company website.
c we need to invest in new equipment.
d get in touch with the local press straight away.
e the launch your top priority?
f is to set up a focus group.

Listen to five people talking about briefings. What do they advise? Write one letter (A–H) next to each number.

1 ☐ D
2 ☐
3 ☐
4 ☐
5 ☐

A abandon unproductive briefings
B use visual aids during briefings
C evaluate the briefing
D invite the right people to the briefing
E outline the objectives for the briefing
F train people in briefings skills
G assign clear roles during briefings
H standardise the briefing process

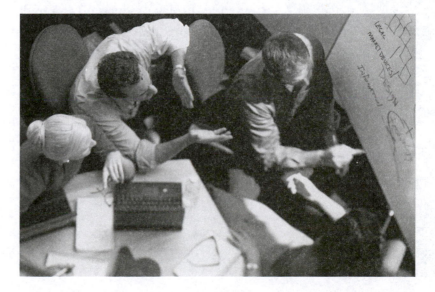

Unit 6 Advertising

Vocabulary:	**Advertising**
Language:	**Gerunds and infinitives**
Career skills:	**Storytelling**
Writing:	**Email responding to an advertisement**

Vocabulary

1 Match the verbs and nouns.

1	project	**a**	an impact
2	target	**b**	an ad
3	make	**c**	an image
4	endorse	**d**	a campaign
5	sponsor	**e**	an event
6	launch	**f**	a brand
7	run	**g**	a launch
8	cancel	**h**	an audience

2 Use the clues to find the words in the puzzle.

1 large advertising sign, usually outdoors
2 fair where companies exhibit their products
3 getting the best results without spending too much money
4 an advert shown on television
5 method of selling over the phone
6 means of making sure that people know about a new product
7 where businesses show what they do or sell
8 shiny and expensive-looking
9 activity to help sell a product
10 used to display products on at a trade show
11 company that provides advertising services to other businesses

3 Complete the table below.

	verb	noun
1	*exhibit*	exhibition
2	reduce	
3	promote	
4		endorsement
5	publicise	
6		persuasion
7	demonstrate	
8		cancellation

Language check

Complete the sentences using the correct form (gerund or infinitive) of the word in brackets.

1 (achieve) results is all my boss cares about.   *Achieving*
2 It's important (present) a professional image of the company and its brands.
3 I look forward to (work) with you on the new campaign.
4 My agent made me (publicise) the new HollyBank soap range, although I can't stand it!
5 I've persuaded two local celebrities (attend) the launch.
6 Can you ask Sam about (set) up the stand?
7 I'm slowly realising that (target) the right people isn't going to be easy.
8 You'll need (liaise) with the manager over the in-store displays.
9 Unfortunately, (cancel) the launch has cost us far more than we'd anticipated.

Listening 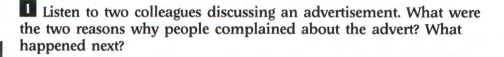 T8

1 Listen to two colleagues discussing an advertisement. What were the two reasons why people complained about the advert? What happened next?

2 Listen again and tick the useful phrases for storytelling you hear.

a It turned out ☐
b You'll never believe it ☑
c To cut a long story short ☐
d Just then ☐
e In the end ☐
f At that very moment ☐
g To get to the point ☐
h Guess what happened next? ☐

1 Read the article quickly and choose the most appropriate title.

New approach fails

Too many ads!

Advertising report findings

Dramatic sales increase

2 Now put the letters in brackets in the correct order to make words from the unit.

3 What do these figures from the article refer to?

a 59   *percentage of people who don't think ads relate to them*

b 3,000

c less than half

d $^1/_3$

e 23

f 2,000

The Economist

Special report

People are tiring of ads in all their forms. A recent study by Yankelovich partners, an American consultancy, says that resistance to the growing intrusiveness of (¹ kartemgni) _marketing_ and advertising has been pushed to an all-time high.

Its study found 65% of people now feel "constantly bombarded" by ad messages and that 59% feel that ads have very little relevance to them.

It has been calculated that the average American is subjected to some 3,000 advertising messages every day.

If you add in everything from the badges on cars to (² nagsols) on sweatshirts, the ads in newspapers, on taxis, in subways, computer pop-ups and even playing on TVs in lifts, then some people could be exposed to more than that number just getting to the office. No wonder many (³ nsucorsem) seem to be developing the knack of tuning-out adverts.

"People are getting harder to influence as (⁴ immeoccrla) clutter invades their lives," says a recent report by Deutsche Bank. It examined the effectiveness of TV advertising on 23 new and mature (⁵ dsbrna) of packaged goods and concluded that in some cases it was a waste of time.

The (⁶ ctffeeevisens) of advertising is a hugely controversial area. Conventional wisdom in the industry is that sales may well increase for a certain period even after the advertising campaign ends, but there comes a point when sales start to decline and it then becomes extremely expensive to rebuild the brand.

This supports the idea of continuous advertising. But some people in the industry believe the conventional wisdom is no longer true. When America's big TV networks reached prime-time (⁷ nsceaduei) of 90% of households, they were a powerful way to build a brand. Now that those groups might be as low as one-third of households, other ways of (⁸ mtogniorp) a brand have become more competitive. Moreover, many clients never really embraced continuous advertising: when times get tough, just as they did in 2000, one of the first things many companies cut is their ad (⁹ dubteg).

Robert Shaw, a visiting professor at the Cranfield School of management in Britain, says that the return from traditional ad (¹⁰ demai) has always been poor. Generally under half of ads provide a return on their investment. And there can be various reasons why ads influence sales, other than their direct effect on consumers. For instance, if a producer announces a multi-million dollar ad (¹¹ ngaipcam) then retailers are often persuaded to increase deliveries. This can result in a "distribution effect" that leads to additional sales.

1 Listen to a news report on Procter and Gamble. Make notes on:

1 What was Tremor?
2 What are early adopters?
3 What are prosumers?

2 Read the audioscript on page 81 and add to your notes. Using your notes, prepare a short (one minute) presentation to give to some advertising students, describing the three groups of people in Exercise 1.

⊙ T10   **3** Listen to the suggested presentation and compare your answer.

Writing   Write an email (60–80 words) to Geoff at Ads4you to ask for a free subscription. Provide the information requested.

Then compare your answer with the suggested answer on page 91.

Ads4you

We are the leading magazine for the advertising industry, offering up-to-date news, resources, job vacancies and so much more.

Email Geoff at ads4you@ee.com to get your free two-week subscription. Remember to tell us what you do, who you work for and why you'd like the subscription – and, of course, where you saw this ad!

Unit 7 Law

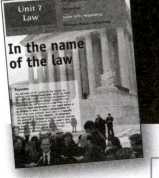

Vocabulary:	**Law**
Language:	**The passive**
Career skills:	**Negotiating**
Writing:	**Email to follow up a meeting**

Vocabulary

1 **Which is the odd one out in each set?**

	a		b		c		d	
1	a	court	b	jury	c	lawyer	d	penalty
2	a	case	b	share	c	bond	d	option
3	a	to sue	b	to litigate	c	to appeal	d	to charge
4	a	conglomerate	b	corporation	c	start-up	d	association
5	a	litigant	b	plaintiff	c	defendant	d	compensation
6	a	outcome	b	verdict	c	settlement	d	trigger

2 **Complete the table below.**

	verb	noun
1	*to patent*	patent
2	to proceed	
3		prosecution
4	to withdraw	
5	to accuse	
6		assessment
7	to permit	
8	to dismiss	

3 **Complete the sentences with these verbs.**

leak   sustain   rule   file   resolve

1 We're going to ___file___ against Melkon shortly.

2 My client _____ terrible injuries in an accident at her workplace three months ago.

3 The judge rarely _____ in favour of the defendant in cases such as these.

4 Do you know who _____ the confidential documents to the press last week?

5 We need to hire a legal expert to help us _____ this dispute.

4 Complete the sentences with the correct options a–c.

1 Litigation __a__ are hard to analyse.
   a risks   b awards   c failures

2 This is the worst case of copyright _____ that I have had to deal with.
   a practice   b conduct   c infringement

3 If the situation doesn't change, we will need to think about taking _____ action.
   a legal   b litigant   c law

4 We're going to take criminal _____ against BRY International.
   a protection   b proceedings   c negligence

5 We need to establish whose intellectual _____ the publication is.
   a property   b failure   c prosecution

6 Hopefully we'll be able to _____ the case out of court.
   a suffer   b sue   c settle

7 Lawyers' _____ can be a substantial amount of the final settlement.
   a proposals   b fees   c actions

8 The plaintiff was awarded $300,000 in _____ .
   a incentives   b damages   c procedures

9 Everyone was very surprised by the guilty _____ .
   a verdict   b judge   c attorney

Language check

Put the sentences in the correct order to make a negotiation with a printer.

a That's out of the question. For a start, we may not have that much printing work coming up in the near future. ☐

b I think you can do better than that. Make it 8% and you've got a deal. ☐

c So, here's what we have in mind. If you guarantee to give us £10,000 worth of business until the end of the year, we'll give you 10% off all your printing costs. [1]

d Done. ☐

e In that case, perhaps we could offer you a 7% discount on all the future work we do for you. ☐

Now write a short email (40–60 words) to the printer you met:

- referring to your previous meeting with him/her
- summarising the deal you both made
- requesting a quote for reprinting your company's annual report.

Then compare your answer with the suggested answer on page 92.

---

1 **Read the article about new legislation. What companies are mentioned in the article? How is each one dealing with the requirement to reduce electronic waste?**

2 **Now complete the article using the active or passive form of the verb in brackets. Use the appropriate tense.**

The Economist

Business

Give us your tired computers

A new plan to restore old PCs may forestall regulation

THE computer industry (1 build) _is built_ on the assumption that PCs and electrical devices (2 replace) _____ every few years. It is a strategy that leaves tons of electronic junk in its wake (over 130,000 PCs every day in America alone). Also, only a tenth or so (3 recycle) _____ . Ingredients such as cadmium, mercury and lead can do terrible things to people and places. In Europe, such e-waste is the fastest growing type of refuse. This (4 account) _____ for 8% of all municipal rubbish.

Regulators (5 take) _____ note. In California, legislation to levy a surcharge on computer sales to defray recycling costs (6 come) _____ into effect last month.

(A European Union directive in 2003 requires equipment-makers to recycle, but it (7 not yet implement) _____ in national laws.) Manufacturers such as IBM, Dell and HP (8 currently try) _____ to deflect further legislation by introducing their own recycling programmes. But they (9 have) _____ limited success – partly because they tend to charge for recycling unwanted machines. Apple's price for taking back one of its computers in America is $30.

Now eBay, the world's leading online auction business, (10 come) _____ up with an innovative way to encourage people to sell, donate or recycle their old machines over the internet. A web-based program "reads" the redundant computer's components and gives its specifications (like its memory and processor speed). Owners can then ascertain the value of their old PC, put it up for sale and get a special mailing kit to simplify shipping. The site also makes it easy to donate a PC to charity or get it to a nearby recycler.

1 **What do you know about WorldCom? Listen to an American TV presenter speaking about WorldCom and answer the questions.**

1   What crime is mentioned?   *fraud*
2   How has the boss hindered prosecutors?
3   Which company is WorldCom compared with and why?

2 **Now look at the audioscript on page 82. Find words with these meanings.**

1   to do with law   *legal*   4   lawyers seeking to prove guilt
2   not innocent   5   to charge
3   financial deception   6   financial ruin

Reading 2

1 **Read the article about American law. Complete the article using these words.**

lawyers   regulators   lawsuit   debt   risks   bribes   fraud   litigation

2 **Read the article again. Are the statements *true* or *false*?**

1   Non-American companies fail to understand they are subject to American law.   *false*
2   A high proportion of SEC-registered companies has been taken to court in the US.
3   Parmalat has moved most of its operations to South America.

The Economist

Business

All American now?

The global spread of US legal risk

Foreign firms that come to America to sell shares and bonds have long understood, at least in theory, that they face the scrutiny of American [1] _regulators_, public prosecutors and its ravenous trial [2]_____. Exploiting these anxieties, American insurance firms began selling policies for directors and corporate officers worldwide as far back as the late 1980s.

Today this threat no longer seems primarily theoretical. Since 1995, according to PriceWaterhouseCoopers, an accounting firm, over 100 foreign firms in America have been sued in private [3]_____. Recent settlements have involved Daimler Chrysler (for $300m), Alcatel ($75m) and Baan ($33m). Both the Securities and Exchange Commission (SEC) and the Department of Justice (DOJ) have investigated Ahold, a Dutch retailer which suffered accounting [4]_____ in its American arm. In fact, calculates Dan Dooley of PriceWaterhouseCoopers, a foreign firm registered with the SEC is a bit more likely to face a [5]_____ in America than an American firm.

These numbers partly reflect the greater globalisation of the world's capital markets, as foreign firms increasingly raise money in America. In 1992, 517 foreign firms were registered with the SEC; in 2002, there were more than 1,300.

But Parmalat, an Italian food and milk-products company which was investigated for falsifying accounts to cover huge losses, is rapidly raising awareness of such jurisdictional [6]_____. Much of Parmalat's [7]_____ mountain was financed by international banks. Bonds ended up in the portfolios of mutual funds, as well as big American life assurance firms, notably AFLAC, which has a reported $428m of exposure. One of the blackest holes is in Brazil, where former finance directors of Parmalat say acquisitions were done at inflated prices, partly to pay [8]_____. And authorities in the Netherlands are investigating how Parmalat's subsidiary there managed to issue €4.45 billion in bonds.

Unit 8 Brands

Vocabulary: Brands
Language: Adjectives and adverbs
Career skills: Dealing with people at work
Writing: Email asking for support

Vocabulary

1 How many nouns related to brands can you find in the word search?

a	i	d	e	n	t	i	t	y	r
w	d	g	f	g	h	m	m	i	a
a	q	w	e	r	t	a	a	z	u
r	g	h	j	k	l	g	n	p	o
e	f	d	s	a	y	e	a	x	c
n	m	n	n	a	m	e	g	b	v
e	p	o	i	u	z	t	e	r	e
s	h	g	f	d	s	a	r	q	w
s	e	x	t	e	n	s	i	o	n
j	k	v	c	m	y	b	a	m	o

2 Complete the table.

	adjective	noun
1	*glamorous*	glamour
2	prestigious	
3	reliable	
4		exclusivity
5	luxurious	
6	popular	
7		effectiveness
8		elegance

3 **Which word is the odd one out in each set?**

	a		b		c		d	
1	a	promote	b	endorse	c	<u>generate</u>	d	advertise
2	a	image	b	campaign	c	brand	d	symbol
3	a	renew	b	revamp	c	retire	d	revive
4	a	conglomerate	b	association	c	corporation	d	accolade
5	a	strategy	b	retailer	c	outlet	d	store
6	a	innovative	b	imaginative	c	creative	d	synonymous

Language check

1 **Complete the sentences with *in, of, towards, up, for, from* or *with*.**

1 Thanks for your ideas. We all approve ___*of*___ your suggestions.
2 Burberry stands _____ tradition and quality.
3 The PR campaign will consist _____ three key elements.
4 The company Fashion-in has succeeded _____ breaking into the UK market.
5 Before stopping for lunch, let's see if we can conjure _____ some ideas for the launch.
6 We're ultimately all working _____ the same goal.
7 The organisation benefited _____ outsourcing its production overseas.
8 The Gucci brand is associated _____ luxury.

2 **Put the words in the correct order to make sentences for dealing with people at work.**

1 on / work / this / let's / together / project
   Let's work together on this project.
2 does / tell / else / to / I / you / wanted / before / anyone
3 the / about / we / know / before / should / start / you / I / think / delay
4 will / his / but / like / I / idea / it / work?
5 just / this / needs / few / changes / a / minor

1 Complete the article below with the following sentences.

a Luxury-goods groups reliant on glamorous names keep high fashion alive.

b Some have merged or tried to cut costs by lowering the quality of their products.

c Today only a handful can afford to carry on.

d Further down the fashion chain things are equally dire.

e Only Chanel is thought to make money.

f The main cause of the mass market's troubles is competition from overseas.

The Economist

Business

Fashion brands today

The sorry state of Europe's rag trade

With a dwindling client base and copies rapidly available from clothes chains with quick production cycles, it has become almost impossible to make money out of exclusive custom-made garments.

The Givenchy and Yves Saint Laurent brands are all making losses, as are Versace and Valentino. [1]___e___ After failing to make a profit for years, Ungaro is on the market. On January 25th, Moët Hennessy Louis Vuitton (LVMH), a luxury-goods firm, sold Christian Lacroix, another loss-making brand, to American duty-free retailers for a "symbolic" price. Prada has parted company with Helmut Lang after persistent losses. Ten years ago, more than 20 houses held Paris shows. [2]_____

Europe's rag trade has been in trouble now for more than five years. [3]_____ Valentino, for example, is owned by Marzotto, Italy's biggest clothing and textile group; Yves Saint Laurent belongs to Pinault-Printemps-Redoute, a French rival to LVMH.

[4]_____ Mass-market producers cannot afford sustained losses. Medium-sized and small companies in France, Italy and Spain are cutting production or moving it abroad. [5]_____ Dozens have already gone under. Many more are streamlining operations and fighting for survival.

[6]_____ Producers cannot match the low labour costs. The effect can be devastating, says Didier Grumbach at the Fédération Française de la Couture, France's main fashion association.

And it can only get worse.

2 Look at the article again. Make notes on the high-fashion brands listed in the table below.

	Brand	Notes
1	Christian Lacroix	*has been sold by LVMH*
2	Versace	
3	Chanel	
4	Prada	
5	Ungaro	

3 Look at the article again. Find words with similar meanings.

1 attractive, exciting   *glamorous*
2 high standard
3 seller
4 available only to a few people
5 making a business more efficient

Listening 🔘 T12   **1** Listen to the radio report on hotel brands and choose the most appropriate description.

a It's becoming more difficult to find an independent hotel chain.
b Hoteliers increasingly prefer running hotels to owning them.
c There's never been a better time to enter the hotel business.

2 Now complete the audioscript on page 82 with the following words. Listen and check your answers. Then underline more examples of adjectives and adverbs in the audioscript.

far   internationally   further   easily   recently
original   well-known   obvious   better   upmarket
grim   well   American-owned   more

Writing   **You are involved in a marketing campaign for one of your company's most prestigious brands. Write an email (50–80 words) to a colleague, asking for help with the campaign. Include:**

– information about what you need help with and when

– a request for your colleague to meet you to discuss the work in more detail.

Then compare your answer with the suggested answer on page 92.

Unit 9 Investment

Vocabulary: **Investment**
Language: **Emphasis**
Career skills: **Prioritising**
Writing: **Press release for a bank**

Vocabulary

1 Match the pairs.

1 strategic	a movement
2 venture	b gains
3 stock market	c alliance
4 business	d angel
5 financial	e capitalist
6 business	f portfolio
7 investment	g venture

2 Complete the table below.

	adjective	noun
1	stubborn	*stubbornness*
2		entrepreneur
3	bankrupt	
4		ethics
5	intuitive	
6		risk
7	analytical	
8		diversification

3 Make words with prefixes to complete the sentences.

1 That document pre- _dates_ me. I only started here last June.
2 My colleague's bi _____ . She speaks French and Spanish fluently.
3 The team have under- _____ their budget by about 5%.
4 I'm only half-way through my report. I really under _____ how long it would take.
5 The meeting was pre _____ , and will take place on Friday.
6 The cheque's been post _____ for next Tuesday.
7 I think the shares have been over _____ by about 10%.

4 How many adjectives to describe personal qualities can you find in the word search?

c	a	l	c	u	l	a	t	i	n	g	w
c	i	g	l	j	k	p	k	p	g	r	c
i	l	a	h	l	f	j	v	r	k	e	i
j	f	j	a	o	s	t	h	u	s	e	t
m	t	o	b	f	z	b	w	d	g	d	s
r	e	c	k	l	e	s	s	e	k	y	i
e	i	d	c	p	t	q	y	n	s	q	m
l	c	i	t	s	i	m	i	t	p	o	i
o	p	i	n	i	o	n	a	t	e	d	s
i	m	h	m	h	k	u	g	s	u	h	s
f	o	c	u	s	e	d	h	j	y	v	e
l	d	e	n	i	m	r	e	t	e	d	p

1 Put the words in the correct order to make useful phrases for prioritising.

1 for / about / forget / that / now

   Forget about that for now.

2 get / Maxine / let's / to / attend / conference / the

3 might / useful / be / it / but / we / have / if / only / time

4 really / do/ the / we / ought / to / review / urgently

5 is / next / the / step / to / new / staff / recruit

6 absolutely / is / the / meeting / deadline / imperative

2 Correct the errors in these sentences.

1 The assessment of the risks has shown is that the procedure needs reviewing.

   What the assessment of the risks has shown ...

2 On no account you should falsify the accounts.

3 Rarely I have faced so much pressure.

4 Never my boss has asked me to give my opinion.

5 Not only we exceeded expectations, but we also made a record profit.

6 What our reinvestment trust provides affordable loans to small businesses.

7 Under no circumstances, companies should be afraid to ask for help.

Read about entrepreneurial activity in different parts of the world. In some lines there is an extra word. Underline the incorrect word or write CORRECT next to the line number.

Enterprising rising

0	Entrepreneurial activity, badly hit by <u>only</u> the bursting of the dotcom bubble,
CORRECT 00	rose strongly last year in both America and Britain. According to a recent
1	study of any 40 countries, the Japanese also became more entrepreneurial
2	in 2003, although such enterprise was even unchanged in Germany
3	and fell sharply in France. An entrepreneur is not defined as anyone
4	creating or is running a start-up company (less than three months old)
5	or a baby business (four to 42 months). A random sample of people
6	aged 18–64 were surveyed to produce an index of total entrepreneurial activity
7	for each country. Because the opportunity, or need, to be entrepreneurial
8	can be differ sharply between countries, particularly between rich and
9	poor countries, comparisons are extreme tricky. In 2003, America was the
10	most entrepreneurial country, with which some 11.9% of 18–64-year-olds
11	entrepreneurs. Uganda had the highest such proportion of entrepreneurs
	of all: 29.2%.

You work for a PR agency. You have been asked to write a press release for a bank, to advertise:

- their strong financial performance over the last 12 months
- their commitment to ethical investment
- a new investment opportunity for customers.

Write 180–220 words. Then compare your answer with the suggested answer on page 92.

1 Steve Walker of ART (Aston Reinvestment Trust) is interviewed about the decisions he has made during his career. Listen and choose the correct options a–c.

1 ART helps businesses that have   *c*
  a faced financial ruin more than once.
  b failed to come up with a good business plan.
  c been refused financial help elsewhere.

2 Steve's best decision has been to
  a take on a team of experienced managers.
  b admit when he needs help from others.
  c work in partnership with similar businesses.

3 Steve advises other companies to
  a work with people from different sectors.
  b set themselves high targets.
  c ask staff to come up with new ideas.

4 ART often works with businesses
  a with a wide range of different difficulties.
  b from the logistics sector.
  c needing help with marketing.

5 How is ART different from a bank?
  a It promotes business development.
  b It offers a lower rate of interest.
  c It has just a few borrowers at a time.

6 What is Steve's worst business decision?
  a investing in a company that went bankrupt
  b listening to a boss's advice
  c wasting time and money on a marketing leaflet

7 Steve learnt from his mistakes the importance of
  a hiring experienced marketing staff.
  b listening to others in the same line of business.
  c using a consultancy agency when required.

8 Steve stresses that businesses should
  a be open to new ideas.
  b expand as quickly as possible.
  c include staff in the decision-making process.

2 Now complete these phrases to summarise what Steve says. (You do not need to use his exact words.)

1 Steve's company, ART, ___*provides affordable loans to small businesses.*___

2 He is happy about his decision to _____

3 Steve regrets _____

4 He would advise other companies to _____

Unit 10 Energy

Unit 10
Energy

What if … ?

Vocabulary: **Energy**
Language: **Conditionals**
Career skills: **Problem-solving**
Writing: **Letter entering a competition**

Vocabulary

1 **Replace the words and phrases in *italics* with words of similar meanings.**

1 Companies are being encouraged to develop *alternative* r<u>enewable</u> energies.

2 A steep rise in the price of oil could be *devastating* c_____ for large numbers of businesses.

3 Energy companies claim there is currently no *lack* s_____ of oil.

4 The increase in energy *use* c_____ is resulting in high levels of pollution throughout the world.

5 The price of *getting oil out of the ground* e_____ looks set to soar.

6 Many countries are *reliant* d_____ on fossil fuels.

7 We need to find new *origins* s_____ of energy.

8 What will be the *effects* c_____ of limited oil supplies?

9 Reserves will be *used up* d_____ within the next 20 years, experts predict.

10 *Discharge* e_____ of waste chemicals have never been so high.

2 **Match the adjectives to the prefixes to form their opposites.**

legitimate regular negotiable possible rational sustainable partial valid renewable legal significant acceptable

un- _sustainable_
_____

non- _____
_____

il- _____
_____

im- _____
_____

in– _____
_____

ir- _____
_____

Language check

1 Some of these conditional sentences contain mistakes. Find and correct the mistakes.

1 What will happen if I ~~would be~~ *'m* late for the conference?
2 If you hadn't reminded me about the meeting, I hadn't gone.
3 We would use solar energy if it was more widely available.
4 If fluorescent bulbs were cheaper, I'm sure more people use them.
5 What you would do if there wasn't such a good bus service?
6 If the company hadn't given employees a free travel pass, staff wouldn't use public transport at all.
7 If someone's already bought me a ticket, then of course I go to the show.
8 If everything had gone according to plan, we would have finished the project yesterday.

2 Complete the gaps in each of these short dialogues using an appropriate phrase.

1 A: How do you suggest we deal with the problem of recruitment?
  B: Let's just take it one step _at a time_.
2 A: How are things going with the IT project?
  B: Great. Couldn't _____ !
3 A: _____ schedule?
  B: Actually we're a few weeks ahead.
4 A: _____ the problem is?
  B: It looks like we've run out of supplies.
5 A: What's the best way to fix this?
  B: If the worst _____, we could always call the maintenance contractors.
6 A: _____ things up?
  B: There's no sign of the delivery van.

1 Listen to five speakers. Match what each one is speaking about to one of these topics.

a   a plan   [1]
b   a concern   [   ]
c   a process   [   ]
d   a presentation   [   ]

e   a solution   [   ]
f   a prediction   [   ]
g   a report   [   ]

2 Now use words from the audioscript on page 84 to complete the table.

	Adjective	Noun
1	sustainable	sustainability
2		affordability
3		alternative
4	ventilated	
5		reliability
6	waste	
7		accessibility
8	dependent	

Writing   You see the poster below on a noticeboard in your workplace. Write a letter (200–250 words) to EnergyFix and enter the competition.

Energy-saving competition!

Save energy and win $5,000

✔   Do you recycle packaging?
✔   Do you turn off the lights at night?
✔   Do you encourage staff to leave their cars at home?

Write to us, EnergyFix, at the address below and tell us what your business does to reduce the amount of energy it uses – and you could win $5,000 to spend on a new energy-saving idea at your company. Tell us what you already do and how you would spend the money. It's that easy!

Then compare your answer with the suggested answer on page 93.

1 Read the article about an environmentally-friendly building. Then complete each of the gaps with an appropriate word.

2 Now answer these questions about the article.

1 Why is the building called 'the Gherkin'?

because of its distinctive, curved shape

2 What is remarkable about the building?

3 What do the figures 65%, 30% and 36% refer to?

4 What is the 'green architecture movement'?

5 What are the benefits of 'green architecture'?

The Economist

Reports

The rise of the green building

Reducing the environmental impact of new buildings

It is officially known ¹___*as*___ the Swiss Re Tower, or 30 St Mary Axe. But Londoners universally refer ²_____ the newest addition to their skyline as "the Gherkin", thanks to the 41-storey building's distinctive, curved profile, which actually looks more like a pine cone. ³_____ is most remarkable about the building is not its name or its shape, however, ⁴_____ its energy-efficiency. Thanks to its artful design and some fancy technology, it is expected to consume ⁵_____ to 50% less energy ⁶_____ a comparable conventional office building. Most people are not used ⁷_____ thinking of large buildings as vast, energy-guzzling machines. But that is what they are. In America, buildings account ⁸_____ 65% of electricity consumption, 36% of total energy use and 30% of greenhouse-gas emissions. So making buildings ⁹_____ energy-efficient could have a significant impact ¹⁰_____ energy policy, notes Rebecca Flora of the Green Building Alliance, a group that promotes sustainable architecture. That is a key goal of the "green architecture" movement, ¹¹_____ is changing the way buildings are designed, built and run.

Proponents of green architecture argue that the approach has many benefits. In ¹²_____ case of a large office, for example, the combination of green design technology can not ¹³_____ reduce energy consumption and environmental impact, but also reduce running costs, create a more pleasant working environment, improve employees' health and productivity, reduce legal liability, and boost property values and rental returns.

Unit 11 Going public

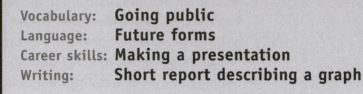

Vocabulary:	**Going public**
Language:	**Future forms**
Career skills:	**Making a presentation**
Writing:	**Short report describing a graph**

Vocabulary

1 Which is the odd one out in each set?

	a		b		c		d	
1	a	stocks	b	<u>accounts</u>	c	equities	d	options
2	a	investor	b	analyst	c	adviser	d	consultant
3	a	pioneer	b	entrepreneur	c	risk-taker	d	manager
4	a	outmanoeuvre	b	outscore	c	outstay	d	outperform
5	a	rational	b	corrupt	c	fair	d	unbiased
6	a	handle	b	manage	c	direct	d	comply
7	a	offering	b	brokerage	c	fee	d	commission
8	a	grow	b	increase	c	diminish	d	expand
9	a	acquire	b	receive	c	obtain	d	repay
10	a	collaboration	b	alliance	c	partnership	d	customer
11	a	auction	b	racket	c	deception	d	corruption

2 Match the words with similar meanings.

1	initial public offering	a	control
2	monopoly	b	revolutionise
3	regulation	c	flotation
4	share	d	cartel
5	reform	e	Securities Exchange Commission
6	stock exchange	f	stake

3 Use the clues to find the words in the puzzle.

1 value of an individual's or a company's assets
2 make a financial guarantee
3 money owed to someone else
4 reveal information
5 payment made to an agent or broker
6 a price reduction

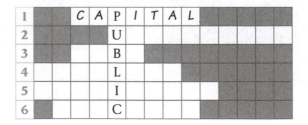

4 Match the pairs.

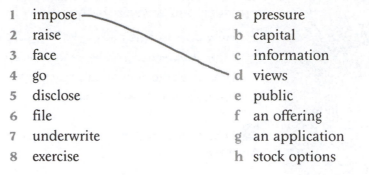

1	impose	a	pressure
2	raise	b	capital
3	face	c	information
4	go	d	views
5	disclose	e	public
6	file	f	an offering
7	underwrite	g	an application
8	exercise	h	stock options

5 Complete the sentences with *on, with, to, for, at* or *into.*

1 We've recently introduced our shares ____*on*____ the stock exchange.

2 It's essential for the company to comply _____ all SEC requirements.

3 Capital in the region of $3m will be available _____ growing the business.

4 Access _____ our helpline is open to all kinds of businesses.

5 In order to provide a good service, we rely _____ a huge team of trained staff.

6 The company was founded _____ three values: trust, enterprise and creativity.

7 If I offer you the shares _____ a 5% discount, are you interested?

8 We're looking at a huge loss, one that could easily run _____ millions.

Language check   Underline the correct verb forms.

1 I'm sure our company *is going / will have gone* public by the end of the year.

2 The IPO *is going / goes* ahead despite rumours to the contrary.

3 I'll check the details again before I *will file / file* the application.

4 The company *may take on / may have taken* on new staff after the forthcoming merger.

5 As soon as I*'m going to hear / hear* from you, I'll get in touch with the auditors.

6 Who *manages / is managing* the auction tomorrow?

7 I can confirm that the meeting with the accountant *is going to start / may start* at ten. Please be prompt.

8 I definitely *won't be buying / might not buy* any shares in Manleys.

9 All employees *will receive / are receiving* about $1,000 when the company goes public.

10 We *are going to invite / invite* all staff to the launch next month.

1 **Listen to Part 1 of a presentation about the services Google provides and answer the questions.**

1 How does Google make a lot of its money?

   through advertising (using an auction approach)

2 How does the auction approach work?

3 What service does AdSense provide?

2 **Listen to Part 2 and make notes on the three new services to Adsense.**

	services	notes
1	marketing	
2	pricing	
3	animated ads	

3 **Listen again and tick the phrases you hear.**

for instance ✓	to put it in simple terms
in other words	i.e.
in brief	I'll come back to that later
as you can see here	let's move on to
to go on to (the next point)	as this chart shows
to sum up	this brings me to
such as	another way of putting that

Writing

Write a short description (60–80 words) describing the changes in the share price at eBay, based on the graph. Then compare your answer with the suggested answer on page 93.

From the beginning
eBay share price, $

Source: Thomson Datastream

Read the article about Google and complete the gaps with these sentences.

a In 1999, some 150m people worldwide used the internet; today, over 1 billion use it regularly.

b The hype and hysteria that accompanied every new scheme to build market share through first-mover advantage is over.

c For instance, PartyGaming, a gambling website, is working on an initial public offering (IPO) that values the firm at about $10 billion.

d But the deal failed to live up to expectations.

e For now it seems inconceivable that it, or a big competitor, might disappear.

f And like numerous other internet firms that were once worth a fortune despite making no money, it is now actually turning a tidy profit.

g Its shares are now worth $285 apiece, three times more than at its IPO last August.

The Economist

Global agenda

An echo of a boom?

Dotcom shares are booming again.

REMEMBER etoys.com? What about Webvan.com? Do Boxman.com or Boo.com ring any bells? Pets.com, perhaps? The casualties of the dotcom bust have long closed or changed hands since the heady days of the late 1990s turned to the crash of the new millennium. But of the internet firms that survived, many are now enjoying soaring market values as investors regard online enterprises with renewed confidence. And new firms are coming to market too, amid no small amount of excitement. [1] _c_

This week Google's share price rose to take the firm's imputed market capitalisation to just above $80 billion, pushing the internet search engine past Time Warner to become the world's most valuable media company. [2]_____ That Time Warner has been overtaken by an online upstart is symbolic for the growing band of sceptics who detect a return to the overvaluation and hype of the tech-bubble days.

Time Warner was involved in the most disastrous merger of the period, when in 2000 it joined forces with America Online. Fans of the deal said that AOL would drag the staid but solid media giant into the new business age. [3]_____ The renamed AOL Time Warner's colossal valuation melted away as the bubble burst. A couple of weeks ago, Time Warner (tellingly, the AOL has gone from the name) was said to be considering a spin-off of its underperforming web-based partner, so bringing the ill-fated venture to a close.

But those who would draw parallels between then and now should note that much has changed since the tech revolution faltered five years ago. Investors, battered by the stockmarket crash that accompanied the demise of the dotcoms, are now a little wiser. Certainly they are unlikely to hand over considerable sums of cash to any online "entrepreneur" with a half-baked business plan. [4]_____ These days, the online giants such as Google, Amazon, MSN, Yahoo! and eBay operate in a different business climate. Since the bursting of the dotcom bubble consumers have logged on to the internet in increasing numbers and have become more comfortable conducting business online. [5]_____ And those who venture into cyberspace are more willing to spend money there.

So in many ways the hopes for the internet of the dotcom boom years are now coming to fruition. Yahoo!, which peaked at a market value of $125 billion in early 2000, had slumped to $4 billion by late 2001. Now it is worth $52 billion. [6]_____ : $849m after tax, on revenues of $3.6 billion, in 2004. Google itself enjoyed revenues of $3.2 billion last year and made a profit of $400m. But they are still far behind the biggest "old media" companies.

Undoubtedly, today's big online ventures are on a surer footing than those that fell in the last dotcom crash. They are being run like proper companies. And there is a bigger pool of customers willing and eager to pay for their services. "Google" has even entered the language as a useful verb for describing a web search. [7]_____ But there is little doubt that Google's valuation looks suspiciously frothy. Do investors in internet stocks really need reminding that what shoots up can just as easily come crashing down?

Unit 12 Competition

Vocabulary:	**Competition**
Language:	**Time clauses**
Career skills:	**Handling conflict**
Writing:	**Report on ways to increase market share**

Vocabulary

1 Match the pairs.

1	niche	a	margin
2	corporate	b	share
3	profit	c	strategy
4	market	d	computer
5	personal	e	market
6	distribution	f	player
7	competitive	g	network
8	mass	h	advantage

2 Complete each of these sentences with one word.

1 I'm sorry, Janice, but you ___*have*___ no right to say that.

2 Ian, can we set _____ our differences, for the sake of the project?

3 If I'm honest, I really don't see what all the fuss is _____ . We've done it before.

4 Let's _____ another go at finding a solution.

5 Gill, what are your views _____ the two models?

6 I know we don't see eye _____ eye on the budget, but are you happy with everything else?

7 _____ you like it or not, Max will be involved in the discussions.

8 Let's keep things _____ perspective. It will only be a short-term venture.

3 Which word is the odd one out in each set?

	a		b		c		d	
1	a	hip	b	fashionable	c	trendy	d	<u>animation</u>
2	a	scanner	b	user	c	computer	d	printer
3	a	impose	b	unveil	c	disclose	d	reveal
4	a	give up	b	abandon	c	cede	d	control
5	a	change	b	evolve	c	adapt	d	release
6	a	attack	b	defend	c	contest	d	fight
7	a	sector	b	rival	c	competitor	d	opposition
8	a	mainstream	b	widespread	c	niche	d	mass
9	a	profits	b	revenues	c	sales	d	positions
10	a	expand	b	grow	c	dabble	d	enhance

1 Read the article about Toyota and underline the correct word or phrase in italics.

The Economist

Special report: Toyota

The car company in front

Pleasing Mrs Jones

Spend some time with Toyota people and after a time you [1] *realise* / *are realising* / *will have realised* / *have realised* there is something different about them. [2] *Like* / *As* / *While* / *By the time* the rest of the car industry raves about engines, gearboxes, acceleration, fuel economy, handling, ride quality and sexy design, Toyota's people talk about "The Toyota Way" and about customers. In truth, [3] *until* / *once* / *as* / *whenever* it is written down the Toyota creed reads much like any corporate mission statement. But it seems to have been absorbed by Japanese, European and American employees alike.

Mr Cho thinks something of [4] *the* / *–* / *a* / *an* unique Toyota culture comes from the fact that the company grew up in one place, Toyota City, 30 minutes drive from Nagoya in central Japan, where the company has four assembly plants surrounded by the factories of suppliers. In this provincial, originally rural setting, Toyota workers in the early days would often have small plots of land that they tended after they [5] *have finished* / *to finish* / *will finish* / *finished* their shift. Mr Cho, who made his career in the company by being a pupil of Mr Ohno and becoming a master of production control, thinks that the fact that Toyota managers and their suppliers see each other every day makes for a sort of hothouse culture – rather like Silicon Valley in its early days.

Jim Press is boss of Toyota's sales in North America. He left Ford in frustration 35 years [6] *ago* / *yet* / *since* / *for*, because he did not think it handled customer relations properly and he suspected that the upstart Japanese company making its way in the American market might do better.

He was right. Toyota shares a production plant in California with GM. [7] *Until* / *By the time* / *As soon as* cars come off the line, some are badged as GM, the rest as Toyotas: after five years, according to one study by Boston Consulting Group, the trade-in value of the Toyota was much more [8] *as* / *like* / *that* / *than* that of the American model, thanks to the greater confidence people had in the Toyota dealer and service network.

Mr Press talks with a quiet, almost religious, fervour about Toyota, [9] *only* / *while* / *as* / *without* mentioning cars as such. "The Toyota culture is inside all of us. Toyota is a customer's company," he says. "Mrs Jones is our customer; she is my boss. Everything is done to make Mrs Jones's life better. We all work for Mrs Jones."

But not even the combination of its world-leading manufacturing, rapid product development and obsessional devotion to customer satisfaction is enough to explain Toyota's enduring success. There is one more ingredient that adds zest to all these. Tetsuo Agata doubles as general manager of Toyota's Honsha plant in Toyota City and as the company's overall manufacturing guru. The magic of Toyota's winning culture was summed up for him by an American friend who observed that Toyota people always put themselves "outside the comfort zone": [10] *until* / *while* / *before* / *whenever* they hit one target, they [11] *set* / *will set* / *are setting* / *have set* another, more demanding one. That relentless pursuit of excellence certainly explains much of [12] *who* / *what* / *where* / *when* has been happening to the company in recent years, at home and abroad.

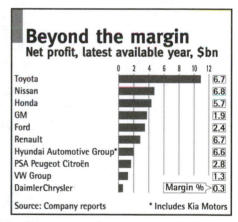

Beyond the margin
Net profit, latest available year, $bn

	$bn
Toyota	6.7
Nissan	6.8
Honda	5.7
GM	1.9
Ford	2.4
Renault	6.7
Hyundai Automotive Group*	6.6
PSA Peugeot Citroën	2.8
VW Group	1.3
DaimlerChrysler	Margin % > 0.3

Source: Company reports   * Includes Kia Motors

2 Now read the article again and answer the questions.

1 What is different about Toyota staff, compared to those at other car companies?

   They talk about the Toyota Way and about the customer, rather than the car performance or design.

2 What does Mr Cho think about Toyota's culture?

3 Why did Jim Press join Toyota?

4 What does Mr Press think about Toyota's culture?

5 What could be the reasons for Toyota's success?

1 **Listen to a radio interview about consumer power and answer the questions.**

1   How is consumer power influencing business?

It is intensifying competition and improving standards.

2   How is the internet increasing competition?

3   How has the way consumers make decisions changed?

4   How have some companies gained competitive advantage?

2 **Listen again and decide if the statements are *true* or *false*.**

1   Few firms nowadays would claim to be truly customer-focused.   *false*

2   The internet is helping to raise standards.

3   Consumers find it useful to read product reviews online.

4   Companies need to improve the layout of their stores.

5   It's easier than ever to target consumers.

6   Dell leads the field in selling PCs.

7   The popularity of search engines looks set to fall.

Writing

Your company's market share is stuck at 5%. Your boss asks you to come up with some suggestions for increasing this. Using the handwritten notes below, write a proposal (220–250 words) to submit to the management team.

> Lower prices – currently much higher than rivals'
>
> Improve brand awareness – use results of market research to help
>
> Re-position products – decide on niche or mass market

Reading

1 **Read the article about Apple and Intel and choose the most appropriate title.**

Surprising takeover

New best friends

Boost to share price guaranteed

Keeping the status quo

Customers leave in disgust

1 Why did people find this picture surprising?
Because they saw Apple and Intel as arch rivals.

2 What plans did Mr Jobs and Mr Otellini announce?

3 What reasons did Mr Jobs give for making these changes?

4 What will be the impact on IBM? Intel? Apple?

The Economist

Business

Intel considers strategic: mobility and the "digital home", in which computers connect to consumer-electronics devices for new entertainment options.

BEAR hugs between arch rivals are becoming fashionable in the computer industry. Scott McNealy and Steve Ballmer, the bosses of Sun Microsystems and Microsoft, started hugging last year and now can't help themselves whenever they mount a stage together. But many in the industry found the sight of Steve Jobs, the boss of Apple Computer, embracing Paul Otellini, his counterpart at Intel, on June 6th in front of some 3,800 software developers at an Apple conference in San Francisco particularly surprising. After all, for more than two decades Apple and "Wintel", the alliance between Microsoft and Intel, have been a sort of Borg and McEnroe, France and England, Harvard and Yale.

That could soon be history. Mr Jobs and Mr Otellini announced that over the next two years Apple will gradually stop using microprocessors from IBM for its desktop PCs and from Freescale Semiconductor, formerly part of Motorola, for its laptops, and switch to Intel chips. This came as quite a shock to many in the cult-like audience. Here was their hero, Mr Jobs, confessing that the Macintosh OSX, Apple's operating system, has for five years been "leading a secret double life" with Intel, whom they regard as a member of "the dark side". Who else is Mr Jobs seeing on the side these days, some were wondering.

For Mr Jobs, who has been leading Apple into a remarkable resurgence, the change is a matter of unsentimental business logic. He compared Intel's "roadmap" for future chip development to IBM's, he said, and concluded that it was better suited to Apple's plans. IBM has also been lagging in such metrics as clock speed, power consumption and heat generation, and supply delays last year caused Apple some difficulties. IBM also appears to have refused to give Mr Jobs the kind of price discounts he was demanding.

Financially, this is not a big setback for IBM, which has been Apple's partner for a decade. Apple represents less than 1% of IBM's revenues. Besides, IBM has recently won contracts to supply microprocessors for all three next-generation game consoles (which might increasingly double as home media centres and computers as well) – Microsoft's Xbox 360, Sony's Playstation 3, and Nintendo's Revolution. According to Laura Conigliaro, an analyst at Goldman Sachs, these will dwarf the lost Apple business by volume.

For the same reason, the deal is not hugely important to Intel's bottom line. Intel already has about 82% of the world market for PC microprocessors. But Intel does gain kudos. Apple is consistently the most chic and innovative player in the PC industry, especially in two areas that

For Apple the change carries risks. Important software developers such as Microsoft and Adobe have said that they will rewrite their applications to work with the new Apple-Intel architecture, but all other software developers will also have to tweak their code. Ms Conigliaro believes that this is "likely to cause some disruptions" and might scare away some prospective Apple customers for a while.

The main implication, however, is that the old certainties are gone. Just as Apple is embracing Intel and firing IBM, Microsoft has abandoned its old ally Intel in favour of IBM (for its consoles, that is). Suddenly, it seems, everybody is getting into bed with everybody. Think of consumer-electronics giants such as Sony, cable companies such as Comcast, or new internet powers such as Google or Yahoo! and one can imagine a lot more hugging to come.

Unit 13 Banking

Money matters

Vocabulary: **Banking**
Language: **Reference words**
Career skills: **Persuading**
Writing: **Email responding to a request for information**

Vocabulary

1 How many different types of bank can you think of?

microfinance

_____

_____ bank

_____

_____

_____

2 Match the words with the definitions.

1 rating agency
2 venture capital
3 asset management
4 joint venture
5 deposit
6 stock trading

a service offered by banks, etc. to maximise returns on investments
b a business alliance entered into by two or more parties
c part of the sale price paid in order to reserve it
d monitors the credit backing of different forms of public borrowing (e.g. Standard and Poor) 1
e money invested in a project where risk is involved
f buying and selling shares, etc.

3 Match the verbs and nouns.

1 fix   a a policy
2 provide   b interest rates
3 go   c public
4 implement   d cheque books
5 issue   e a transaction
6 carry out   f advice
7 raise   g capital

4 Complete the table.

	verb	noun	person
1	*assess*	assessment	*assessor*
2		——	lender
3			banker
4		loan	——
5	implement		——
6	invest		
7	pay		——
8		recovery	——

5 Match three of these verbs with each noun.

| apply for   make   secure   lend   pay off |
| pull out of   agree   invest   deposit |

a   *apply for*

_____ a loan

_____

b _____

_____ a deal

_____

c _____

_____ money

_____

6 Match the words to the categories.

institution   business   client management   taxation
joint venture   corporation   pension planning   company
corporate debt   agency   portfolio management   merger
takeover   partnership

a Types of organisations:

_____*business*_____   _____

_____   _____

_____

b Types of alliances:

_____*partnership*_____   _____

_____   _____

c Types of banking departments and services:

_____*client management*_____   _____

_____   _____

_____

1 Match the sentence halves.

1 If you don't do it this way, then we'll
2 Bearing all things in mind, I
3 After looking at all sides of the argument,
4 It's in all of our interests
5 Don't forget, we're all
6 Unless you're prepared to pay 50% upfront

a I've decided not to proceed with the project.
b in this together.
c the deal's off.
d have to forget the whole thing.
e to make this work.
f don't think we've done too badly.

2 Complete the sentences with the correct options a–c.

1 Please don't make a habit __c__ coming in so late.
   a on   b for   c of

2 Max is the tax consultant. He's the _____ I was telling you about earlier.
   a such   b one   c the former

3 The second applicant made the best impression _____ me.
   a on   b with   c for

4 I've found six mistakes so far in the report, and _____ are just the ones in the introduction.
   a these   b this   c that

5 Martina has just finished studying business studies. _____ includes administration, HR and finance.
   a One   b This   c Such

6 We've spoken to Intex, RTL Associates and Maxi about merging. _____ seems the most likely.
   a the latter   b these   c ones

Writing

Write an email (100–120 words) in response to Bruce, to follow up your discussions with MTO Bank. Then compare your answer with the suggested answer on page 94.

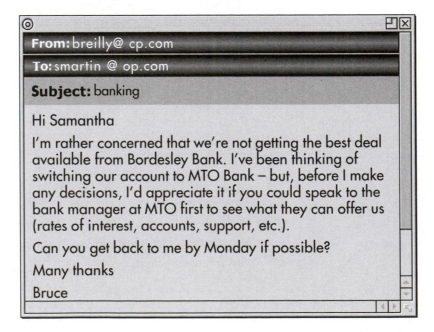

From: breilly@ cp.com
To: smartin @ op.com
Subject: banking

Hi Samantha

I'm rather concerned that we're not getting the best deal available from Bordesley Bank. I've been thinking of switching our account to MTO Bank – but, before I make any decisions, I'd appreciate it if you could speak to the bank manager at MTO first to see what they can offer us (rates of interest, accounts, support, etc.).

Can you get back to me by Monday if possible?

Many thanks

Bruce

Read the article about bank mergers and complete the gaps appropriately.

The Economist

Finance & Economics

European bank mergers

Will an Italian-German marriage encourage others?

BANKERS are not quite expecting a wave of copy-cat mergers across Europe. But the takeover, announced on June 12th [1] __*by*__ UniCredit, Italy's largest bank, of HVB Group, Germany's second-biggest, has set the rumour mills turning. Until this daring marriage, [2] _____ will create continental Europe's fourth-biggest bank, the accepted wisdom had [3] _____ that the mere sniff of a cross-border deal was enough to punish the share prices of both parties. Yet [4] _____ the time Alessandro Profumo, UniCredit's chief executive, and Dieter Rampl, his counterpart at HVB, hugged [5] _____ other in front of cameras in Munich, the German bank's share price had soared, while the Italian one's had [6] _____ least held steady.

Four years ago, [7] _____ Mr Profumo was contemplating a similar deal with Commerzbank, another German bank, the share prices of both plummeted. Last year, Dexia, a Franco-Belgian bank group, and Sanpaolo IMI, its putative Italian partner, saw their shares suffer as investors turned [8] _____ their noses at their merger proposal. Mr Profumo sensed that [9] _____ mood started to change with last year's purchase of Abbey, Britain's sixth-biggest bank, [10] _____ Spain's Santander Central Hispano.

UniCredit will pay around €19 billion ($23 billion) [11] _____ a full takeover of HVB and its listed affiliates, Bank Austria and BPH, a Polish bank. The group will [12] _____ a strong force in northern Italy, Bavaria, Germany's southernmost state, the northern German city of Hamburg, Austria and four countries in central and eastern Europe. About 9,000 jobs are expected to go [13] _____ of overlaps, especially in Poland. In Germany, 2,000 jobs will be lost, but through natural attrition, [14] _____ addition to 2,200 already planned.

Mr Profumo, [15] _____ is set to be the new bank's chief executive, and Mr Rampl, the prospective chairman, argue that the combination of stable business in western Europe and high growth farther east is a good business mix. The new group's biggest challenge will be in Germany, [16] _____ HVB has struggled with a fragmented retail market and a legacy of bad corporate and property loans. Perhaps its biggest weakness is its thin capitalisation: a tier-one capital ratio of just over 5%. That puts it at the bottom end of the range for banks with a market value of €40 billion or more.

---

1 Listen to another bank executive discussing a bank merger and answer the questions.

1 Which two banks are merging?   *UniCredit and HVB*
2 What are the difficulties of the merger?
3 What positive factors may help the merger work?
4 How might Italy's central bank react?
5 What could the future hold for Germany's Commerzbank and for Deutsche?

2 Which of these verbs have the same noun form in the listening?

expand	merge	need	fit	challenge

Unit 14 Training

Vocabulary: **Training**
Language: **Clauses and sentence construction**
Career skills: **Motivating**
Writing: **Press release for a training programme**

1 Match the pairs.

1	staff	a	centre
2	training	b	course
3	in-company	c	development
4	job	d	loyalty
5	case	e	satisfaction
6	professional	f	study

2 Complete the table.

	verb	noun
1	perform	*performance*
2		participation
3	motivate	
4	manipulate	
5		budget
6	achieve	
7		impact
8		customisation

3 Which is the odd one out in each set?

	a		b		c		d
1	a seminar	b tutorial	c class	d format
2	a delegate	b expert	c trainee	d participant
3	a tutor	b trainer	c advisor	d instructor
4	a in-company	b intensive	c in-house	d internal
5	a online	b hands-on	c practical	d interactive
6	a individual	b executive	c customised	d unique
7	a lead	b conduct	c run	d cope
8	a skills	b knowledge	c understanding	d workshop

Language check

1 Complete the sentences with *on*, *in*, *up*, *to*, *with*, *out* or *of*.

1 I couldn't relate ___to___ anything the seminar leader was saying.
2 Have you signed _____ for the presentation skills course yet?
3 You have to comply _____ all the legal requirements.
4 The next session will focus _____ analysing training needs.
5 Let's start by looking at all the options open _____ us.
6 I don't know what the cause _____ this problem is.
7 Few of the courses conform _____ what it says in the brochures.
8 I'll be asking you to act _____ the case study later.
9 The feedback could result _____ a follow-up course being organised.
10 The tutor pointed _____ key features of the case study.

2 Look at these sentences for motivating staff. Find and correct the mistakes.

1 You get the business, you get ^the bonus.
2 Come on. You've got to do better as that!
3 Would you like taking full responsibility for this?
4 I'm going to let you handle with this.
5 We're all in to this together.
6 It's everybody's interests to take on more staff.
7 I offering an additional commission to whoever strikes the deal.
8 This is a last chance to sort things out.

3 Complete the email with appropriate conjunctions to link clauses.

Dear Solveig

I am writing to update you on the training situation here in the Lulford office.

1 ___After___ reviewing a number of local training organisations, we have finally decided on one preferred training provider, MLT Communications. We chose them 2_____ they have an excellent reputation and have received good feedback from delegates. This decision was made 3_____ the fact that a second company, Train4U, offered us a lower price on some courses. 4_____ get things moving, we've asked MLT to conduct the assertiveness training sessions during the spring, 5_____ they are prepared to work out of town at our regional training centre. 6_____ of our decision, we are advising all HR staff to book training for employees through MLT.

1 Listen to part of a radio programme about the Centre for Creative Leadership. Make notes below.

The centre	founded 1970 in North Carolina ...
Typical programmes	
Pre-course tasks	
Approaches to teaching/learning	

2 Find words in the audioscript on page 86 with these meanings.

1 inspire
2 company offering training
3 people who have completed their studies
4 concentrated, very focused
5 class
6 role-play
7 tutor

Read the article about teaching leaders to lead. In some lines there is an extra word. Underline the incorrect word or write CORRECT next to the line number.

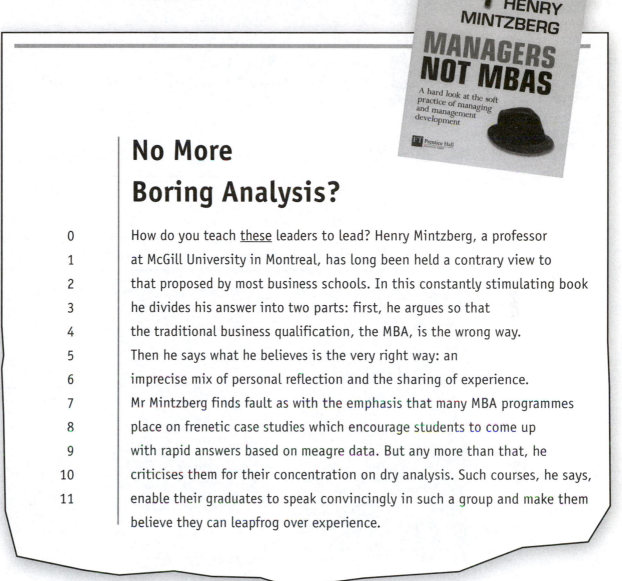

No More Boring Analysis?

0	How do you teach <u>these</u> leaders to lead? Henry Mintzberg, a professor
1	at McGill University in Montreal, has long been held a contrary view to
2	that proposed by most business schools. In this constantly stimulating book
3	he divides his answer into two parts: first, he argues so that
4	the traditional business qualification, the MBA, is the wrong way.
5	Then he says what he believes is the very right way: an
6	imprecise mix of personal reflection and the sharing of experience.
7	Mr Mintzberg finds fault as with the emphasis that many MBA programmes
8	place on frenetic case studies which encourage students to come up
9	with rapid answers based on meagre data. But any more than that, he
10	criticises them for their concentration on dry analysis. Such courses, he says,
11	enable their graduates to speak convincingly in such a group and make them
	believe they can leapfrog over experience.

You work in the PR department of a large training organisation. Write a press release to advertise a new and innovative training programme your company is launching. Give information about the programme (target customers, training approach, content, location, cast, etc.) and how to book a place. Write 180–220 words.

Then compare your answer with the suggested answer on page 95.

Unit 15 Consulting

Vocabulary:	**Consulting**
Language:	**Reported speech**
Career skills:	**Reporting**
Writing:	**Short internal company report**

Vocabulary

1 Complete the word map with the following words.

> restructure   retail   re-organise   clients   regulate   advisor
> professional-service firm   customer   IT   implement   accountant
> legislate   auditing   advise   outsource   consultant   tax
> auditor   SEC   co-ordinate   branding   plan   bookkeeping
> corporate development   multinationals   lawyer   service provider

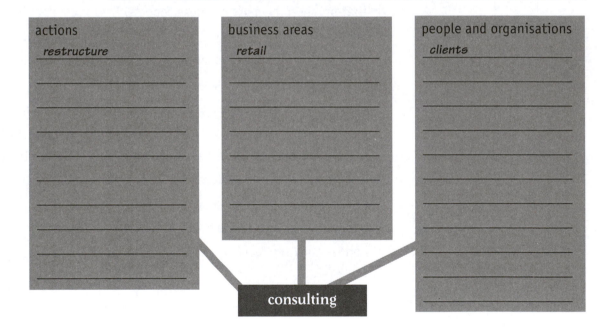

actions
restructure

business areas
retail

people and organisations
clients

consulting

2 Match the verbs and nouns.

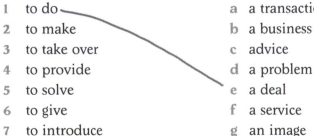

1	to do	a	a transaction
2	to make	b	a business
3	to take over	c	advice
4	to provide	d	a problem
5	to solve	e	a deal
6	to give	f	a service
7	to introduce	g	an image
8	to project	h	legislation
9	to carry out	i	an audit

1 Complete the sentences with one of the options a-d.

1 The strategy you've outlined looks __c__ it might work.

   a as   b if   c like   d then

2 My boss admitted _____ to cancel our meeting.

   a to forget   b forgetting   c forget   d had forgotten

3 One of our clients has invited us _____ their open day.

   a to attend   b attend   c attending   d be attending

4 I would liken Met Consulting _____ our competitor Ridgeley.

   a in   b at   c to   d by

5 The consultants told me that they _____ auditing our department yesterday.

   a have finished   b finish   c are finishing   d finished

6 For the _____ of large consultancy firms like ours, the next two years look extremely challenging.

   a likes   b liken   c like   d to like

7 My colleague _____ the contract last week.

   a warned me not to sign   b warned signing

   c has warned me not to sign   d warned me sign

8 Margot suggested that we _____ the situation carefully over the coming weeks.

   a may monitor   b should monitor

   c have monitored   d had monitored

2 Match the sentence halves.

1	What the CEO wants us to do	a	to take any of the advice.
2	The bottom line is	b	is to pretend everything is OK.
3	We finally agreed to	c	make a quick decision.
4	In short, Cécile is refusing	d	we can't afford to employ any more consultants.
5	I suggest we	e	taking on a new advisor.
6	What Jack was trying to say was	f	that he didn't agree with us.
7	My boss suggested	g	take on another supervisor.

Writing

Write a short internal company report (200–250 words):

– analysing the strengths and weaknesses of your company's products or services (or of a company you know well)

– advising what strategies need to be adopted to stay on top

– suggesting other challenges that lie ahead for your company.

Then compare your answer with the suggested answer on page 95.

1 Listen to Kevin Philipps, from the Mentor Consulting Group, speaking about Nokia. Make notes in the table below.

Problems with products	*Uninspiring – did not address users' desire for more exciting design; reluctant to customise products*
Dealing with problems	
Future challenges	

2 Listen again. Which of these approaches did Nokia use to stay on top?

1	raise shareholder value		6	use local consultants
2	introduce new products	✓	7	restructure its management team
3	rebrand existing models		8	focus on clients' needs
4	reduce costs		9	move into new markets
5	increase production		10	outsource production

Reading **1** Read this extract from a financial consultancy's prospectus and answer the questions.

1 What area of business can cause companies difficulties in their early days?   *Financial management is often …*

2 How can using a consultancy firm help companies?

3 What service does Oakwood offer clients?

Taking the hassle out of finance

Oakwood Financial Management – The complete solution

                        its
Financial management can often be one of the biggest pitfalls for a business in it's initial stages of growth. Whether it is producing tax returns, forecasting the company's financial future or simply managing the day-to-day accounts of the business, this complex and time-consuming aspect of running a successful company can often make or break a growing venture.

Using a reputable and efficient financial consultancy company can provide a company with essential piece of mind when it comes to the financial structuring of this integral part of the company. A good financial advisor will draw upon years of expereience and expertese across a variety of corporate disciplines to not only effectively mange the companys finance, but also instruct and advice on potential investment opportunities, future hurdles the company may encounter and ultimately help the business move forward and, above all, grow.

Oakwood Financial Management was established in 1999. Employing over 30 financial consultants, the company provides tailored advice to create and protect the wealth of over 4,500 domestic and comercial clients spanning a range of areas and industry. Achieving a high level of succes through care, diligence and, above all, the skill of the team, Oakwood maintains a high level of customer-focused service that ensures every client's busness needs are dealt with in both an ethical and profesional manner.

2 Read the extract again. It contains twelve proof-reading mistakes. Find and correct them.

3 Now read a second extract from the consultancy's prospectus. Complete the extract using the noun form of the verbs in brackets.

4 Read the extract again and match each paragraph with one or more of these options.

a   Oakwood gives both private and business financial advice.   [3]

b   The company grew through word of mouth.   ☐

c   Oakwood advises companies not to just ignore problems.   ☐

d   Good planning ensures the success of a business.   ☐

e   Oakwood successfully works with start-up companies.   ☐

f   The company is committed to its future development and that of its customers.   ☐

1   We have worked extremely hard at Oakwood to provide our clients with the most effective financial (¹ advise) _advice_ and (² manage) _____ possible. The fact that we have built the company upon personal (³ recommend) _____ , is testament to the honest, open and impartial way in which we conduct business. Our projected turnover for the forthcoming year is over £2 million and this is a true indication of the dedication that we have – not only to the continued (⁴ succeed) _____ of Oakwood, but also to our clients' businesses.

2   Oakwood can help to deal with the financial pressures of running any growing business. Often it can be difficult to establish the true financial needs of a company because the person in question does not have the necessary (⁵ know) _____ or training to draw upon. Oakwood offers clients access to financial (⁶ consult) _____ who are able to assess and explain the financial concerns and needs of a growing company in order to not only point out where the client needs to take action, but also then push the business forward.

3   All our consultants are highly experienced within the field of commercial finance. Assisting our clients to plan for their futures – in a domestic and a commercial sense – requires us to consider all aspects of their financial well-being. It makes sense for us to take care of all the clients' financial needs, whether they are encompassed within their business or not. We can advise on pensions, loans, (⁷ invest) _____ and any other concern or enquiry our client may have. We are also careful to ensure that we highlight any protection needs or tax-saving opportunities that may exist. This level of service demands the financial planning skills that we have built up over the years, enabling us to fully understand the financial situation and needs of the individual as well as their business.

4   Many business people simply do not fully understand the financial situation that their company is in and this 'stick your head in the sand' approach almost always leads to difficulties in the future. Successfully planning the financial future of the business essentially guarantees future success and further growth. Using a reputable and highly skilled Financial Management company such as Oakwood takes the matter off the agenda. All of the hassle, jargon, (⁸ regulate) _____ and (⁹ legislate) _____ normally associated with financial matters is dealt with by us on the client's behalf, enabling them to get back to the most important matter of all – running their business.

BEC Higher practice test

Introduction to BEC (Business English Certificate) Higher

This workbook contains a complete BEC Higher practice test (on pages 64–78). The BEC Higher examination is a Cambridge ESOL (UCLES) business English examination at advanced level. BEC Higher consists of four components: reading, writing, listening and speaking.

Reading test

Different parts of the Reading paper test different reading skills. Part 1 tests reading for gist and scanning. Part 2 tests your ability to understand text structure; in order to do this you are required to fill a gapped text with sentences. Part 3 tests your ability to read for gist and understand specific information. Part 4 tests your vocabulary. Part 5 tests grammar and understanding of cohesion. Part 6 is a proofreading task, where you are required to identify extra words in a short text.

When preparing for the examination, it is useful to:

– practise reading as many types of documents as you can

– make sure you understand the use of reference words (like *this*, *such* and *it*)

– record useful vocabulary and fixed phrases linked to different business topics

– check your own work and keep a record of the typical mistakes you make

– exchange your written work with a fellow student and check his/her work for errors.

Writing test

The Writing paper tests short neutral/formal writing in Part 1 (describing a graph) and longer neutral/formal writing in Part 2 (letter, report or proposal). It is important in the Writing paper that you:

– answer the question that is set

– use a variety of grammatical structures and vocabulary accurately and appropriately

– make sure that your writing is clear and well structured

– write concisely and pay attention to the suggested number of words.

Listening test

The Listening paper tests a variety of listening skills, for example, listening for gist (identifying topic, context, etc.) in Part 2, and listening for both main ideas and specific information in Part 3. When preparing for the examination you should:

– get as much listening practice as possible

– practise taking notes when you are taking part in meetings, making telephone calls, listening to presentations, etc. (this will help you with Part 1)

– consider the following as you listen to English: who the speakers might be, what their role is, what the purpose of the conversation is, etc.

Speaking test

The Speaking paper tests different skills. In Part 1 you are tested on your ability to talk about yourself (work, interests, etc.). Try to answer the questions as fully as possible.

In Part 2 you choose one of three business topics and give a 'mini-presentation' (for approximately one minute) on the topic. Before you start your presentation, you are given a minute to prepare what you want to say; it is a good idea to make brief notes during this time. At the end of the presentation, the other candidate can ask you a question; give as full an answer as you can. During your presentation, it is important that you:

– outline your main points clearly and refer to them in a logical order

– give reasons for your points.

In Part 3 of the Speaking paper you are asked to discuss a given topic with another candidate. It is important that you:

– give your opinion on the topic and give reasons for your opinions

– ask the other candidate for his/her opinions.

The tables on page 65 describe the components of the BEC Higher examination. The final columns refer you to units with workbook exercises which practise those skills required in the BEC Higher tasks. You may find it useful to focus on them if you are preparing for the examination.

Reading test (60 minutes)

Part	Type of reading	Task	Number of questions	Workbook units
1	Gist and scanning	Matching sentences with texts	8	Unit 15
2	Understanding text structure	Matching sentences with gaps in text	6	Units 1, 8 and 11
3	Gist and specific understanding	Multiple choice comprehension questions	6	Unit 4
4	Vocabulary and structure	Multiple choice gap filling	10	Units 2 and 4
5	Grammar and cohesion	Single word gap filling	10	Units 10 and 13
6	Finding errors	Proofreading (finding extra words)	12	Units 5, 9 and 14

Writing test (70 minutes)

Part	Task	Time	Workbook units
1	Writing a description of a graph	120–140 words	Unit 4, 11
2	Writing a letter, report or proposal	200–250 words	Units 2, 9 and 12

Listening test (40 minutes including 10 minutes to transfer answers to a separate answer sheet)

Part	Type of listening	Task	Number of questions	Workbook units
1	Listening for specific information	Gap filling	12	Unit 1
2	Identifying topic, purpose, etc. of short monologues	Multiple matching	10	Unit 5 and 10
3	Answering questions based on a longer conversation	Multiple choice comprehension questions	8	Unit 3 and 9

Speaking test (15 minutes)

Part	Task	Time	Workbook units
1	Giving information about yourself (work, hobbies, etc.)	About 3 minutes	Unit 1
2	Giving a 'mini-presentation' about a business topic	About 6 minutes	Unit 5
3	Discussion with another candidate on a given topic	About 7 minutes	Unit 3

READING TEST

PART ONE

Questions 1 – 8

- Look at the statements below and at the five extracts from an article about public relations (PR).

- Which extract (**A, B, C, D** or **E**) does each statement (1–8) refer to?

- For each statement **1 – 8**, mark one letter (**A, B, C, D** or **E**).

- You will need to use some of these letters more than once.

> **Example**
>
> Many organisations prefer to delay agreeing on a sponsorship until the latest opportunity.   *E*

1   PR strategies lasting around half a year are the most effective.

2   There isn't always time to involve the press or hold interviews.

3   There are proven advantages of getting PR involved early.

4   There are two main goals to any sponsorship.

5   PR agencies need to be able to respond to last-minute sponsorship.

6   The difficult thing is linking the brand and the sponsorship.

7   Sponsorship is less likely to succeed if a good PR strategy is not in place.

8   The role of PR has changed greatly in recent years.

A
> The most successful sponsorships are those that make PR the lead communications tool. Sponsorship aims to make it famous and to make it work economically for the brand. PR is central to both these aims and should be involved right from the beginning. Currently this is the case in only half of sponsorship strategies. PR needs to get in even before the deal has been signed, where different strategies are being considered. Without viable, well-thought-out PR, the sponsorship has a significantly reduced chance of working.

B
> PR is typically involved only when the sponsoring organisation and the marketplace have been analysed and a sponsorship identified, developed and negotiated. This can mean leveraging a sponsorship with limited opportunities for all the elements, such as personal appearances or media access. A PR consultancy has to demonstrate a high level of knowledge, expertise and insight in order to be an active partner. Doing basic PR is relatively easy, but the challenge lies in tying the brand closely to the sponsorship.

C
> An in-house team is involved from the start of any project, which helps shape the media value of the activity. Several years ago, sponsorship was managed by the events team and PR would be brought in at a much later stage. Having PR fully integrated doubled results. Today's longer lead-time and ability to take part in better strategic conversations are really paying off. We've had more time, which means being able to think outside the normal product placement routes. This has included setting up partnerships and getting coverage from the media.

D
> Even in the highest-profile sponsorships there is the same pressure for word to spread. Nothing truly gets off the ground unless the PR accompanying it is first-rate. The best strategies are those that take anything up to 3–6 months – the longer the better – 'considering every angle before signing a deal'. Of course, sponsors do not always have the time to formulate a considered PR approach. Many deals are signed only weeks before the event occurs, making the role of PR much more limited.

E
> It is precisely the ability of agencies to react to late deals that should also play to their advantage. While preferring early involvement, late deals are something they should also promote themselves as being able to manage. Late sponsorship is a 'nightmare' for advertising as late deals make it difficult to buy media slots. This is a scenario where only PR can make a significant impact. The ability of PR to make an impact close to an event may be a reason why many sponsors still don't consider it until this late stage.

PART TWO

Questions 9 – 14

- Read this text taken from a business magazine.

- Choose the best sentence to fill each of the gaps.

- For each gap **9 – 14**, mark one letter **(A – H)**.

- Do not use any letter more than once.

- There is an example at the beginning, **(0)**.

Spare me the details

There is a huge gap between what consumers want and what vendors would like to sell them. Lisa Hook, an executive at AOL, one of the biggest providers of traditional ('dial up') internet access, has learned amazing things by listening in on the calls to AOL's help desk. **(0)** _H_. The help desk's first question is: 'Do you have a computer?' Surprisingly often the answer is no, and the customer was trying to shove the installation CD into the stereo or TV set. The help desk's next question is: 'Do you have a second telephone line?' Again, surprisingly often the answer is no. This means that the customer cannot get on to the internet. **(9)** .... And so it goes on.

Admittedly, in America, where about half of all internet households now have high-speed ('broadband') connections, these AOL customers are so-called 'late adaptors', or 'analogues'. But even younger, savvier 'digital natives' or 'digital immigrants' can provide surprising insights for those who care to listen.

Genevieve Bell works for Intel, the world's biggest semiconductor-maker. She has been travelling around Asia for three years to observe how Asians use, or choose not to use, technology. **(10)** .... Americans tended to say things like 'my home is my castle' and furnish it as a self-contained playground. Asians were more likely to tell her that 'my home is a place of harmony', 'grace', 'simplicity' or 'humility'. **(11)** ....

Even within Western cultures, Ms Bell, who is Australian, has found startling differences in the way people view technology. **(12)** .... As she did so, she immediately got a mocking 'Oi, what do you think you are, famous?' from the next table. 'For Americans, adopting technology is an expression of American-ness, part of the story of modernity and progress,' says Ms Bell. **(13)** ....

And even Americans, perhaps more prone than others to workaholism, can get frustrated by technology. Chris Capossela, boss of productivity software at Microsoft, commissioned a study where office workers were shadowed (with their consent) after they left the office. **(14)** .... Thanks to technology (laptops, Blackberries, smart phones and so on), he says, 'the boundaries of nine-to-five no longer exist.' This creates a new demographic category, 'the enterprise consumer', for whom not only technology but all of life has grown more complex.

A She recently opened her laptop in a café in Sydney to check her email.

B He or she is, of course, already on the line to the help desk.

C The industry is currently hoping to develop these technologies even further.

D She was especially struck by the differences in how Westerners and Asians view their homes.

E For many other people, it may be just a hassle, or downright pretentious.

F They recoiled from gadgets that made noises or looked showy or intrusive.

G It showed that people feel pressure even in their cars and homes to keep up with the expectation that one is always available.

H Usually, the problem is that users cannot get online.

PART THREE

Questions 15 – 20

- Read the article below about the oil industry.
- For each question **15 – 20**, mark one letter (**A**, **B**, **C** or **D**) for the answer you choose.

Oil in troubled waters

1   The surge in oil prices, from $10 a barrel in 1998 to above $50 in early 2005, has prompted talk of a new era of sustained higher prices. But whenever a 'new era' in oil is hailed, scepticism is in order. After all, this is essentially a cyclical business in which prices habitually yo-yo. Even so, many attending a recent conference pointed to evidence of a new 'price floor' of $30 or perhaps even $40.

2   So, why did prices shoot up in the first place? Oil markets have seen an unprecedented combination of tight supply, surging demand and financial speculation. One supply-side factor is OPEC's (Organisation of the Petroleum Exporting Countries) clever manipulation of output quotas – they decided to raise output just as the South-East Asian economies were hit by crisis, sending prices plunging to $10. Desperate to engineer a price rebound, Saudi Arabia targeted inventory levels: whenever oil stocks in the rich countries of the OECD (Organisation for Economic Cooperation and Development) started rising, OPEC would reduce oil quotas to stop prices softening. It worked like a charm. Another factor has been the shortage of petrol in the American market – prices have spiked as refineries have been unable to meet local demand surges.

3   Adding to the froth has been the sudden influx of new kinds of financial investors into the oil market. Many are merely chasing the huge returns recently offered by oil. Big equity funds, fearful of what $100 oil could do to their holdings, might invest in oil futures at $40 or $50 as a cheap insurance policy. Phil Verleger, an energy economist, reckons that OPEC itself may be to blame for the speculation: by declaring its intention to prop up prices, first at $30 and now at $40, 'OPEC has given Wall Street a free put option' (because investors believe the cartel will cut output to stop prices falling).

4   Supply constraints coincided with a huge boom in oil demand. Global oil consumption last year increased by over 3.4% instead of the usual 1–2%. About 30% of that growth came from China, where oil consumption rocketed by perhaps 16%. One senior European oil executive claims that, in contrast with the embargoes and supply-driven price rises of the past, 'This is the first demand-led oil shock.' And it was not just China that used a lot more oil. India's oil consumption too leapt last year, and America's was quite robust. In fact, despite $50 oil, global oil demand in 2004 grew at the fastest rate in over a quarter of a century.

5   So was it supply or demand that pushed prices above $50? Both matter, of course, but neither provides a complete explanation. What is new is the lack of spare production capacity. In a normal commodity market, no producer would keep lots of idle capacity. But that is what several OPEC countries have been doing for years. Saudi Arabia, in particular, has maintained a generous buffer to prevent the market from overheating during unexpected supply interruptions. Alas, the buffer has been in decline for some years, because OPEC has not been investing sufficiently to keep pace with growing demand. As a result, global spare capacity last year dropped to around 1m barrels per day, close to a 20-year low. Almost all of this was in Saudi Arabia. In short, the market for the world's most essential commodity now has no safety net to speak of.

15 What is said about the oil industry?

   A It is usual to see oil prices fluctuating.

   B A major energy conference is due to take place shortly.

   C Many senior managers fear they will lose their jobs.

   D Several oil companies are being restructured.

16 Which of these has nothing to do with the higher oil price?

   A financial speculation

   B limited supplies

   C global panic

   D rising demand

17 According to paragraph 3, investors

   A are leaving the oil industry in their hundreds.

   B are entering the oil industry to make large profits.

   C think OPEC will reduce oil prices.

   D consider oil to be a high-risk business.

18 Over the last twelve months, consumption of oil

   A has remained the same rate in China and India.

   B has fluctuated in the United States.

   C has been a third higher than in the previous year in Europe.

   D has risen more quickly than in the last 25 years.

19 Which statement is made in paragraph 5?

   A There is now a larger than expected global oil capacity.

   B Oversupply is leading to problems in the oil industry.

   C Saudi Arabia is investing in systems to monitor oil supplies better.

   D OPEC's usual role is to try and keep the supply of oil steady.

20 Which title suits the article best?

   A Why demand for oil has risen

   B Troubled times for the oil industry

   C Oil prices set to soar

   D Charges recede as oil profits fall

PART FOUR

Questions 21 – 30

- Read the article below about consumer electronics.
- Choose the best word to fill each gap from **A, B, C** or **D**.
- For each question **21 – 30**, mark one letter (**A, B, C** or **D**).
- There is an example at the beginning, (0).

Consumer electronics

Another year, another standards war in the consumer-electronics business. After the (0) ...*B*... between VHS and Betamax in the 1970s comes a new saga in which two rival – and, inevitably, (21) .... – formats struggle to establish themselves as the successor to the wildly popular DVD standard. Both new formats rely on blue lasers, which can discern finer details than the red lasers used in DVD players, to squeeze more data on to each disc. This (22) .... can be used in two ways: to (23) .... quality, by providing a more detailed 'high definition' picture, or to increase quantity, (24) .... more footage (at DVD quality) to fit on a single disc.

In one corner is the HD-DVD format, (25) .... by Toshiba, NEC and Sanyo. The details are still sketchy – the technical (26) .... will not be finalised until February – but HD-DVD will offer at least three times the storage of DVD. Proponents of HD-DVD claim the discs can be made cheaply using existing DVD production lines with very little (27) .... The first HD-DVD devices will go on sale next year.

In the other corner is Blu-ray, backed by a (28) .... that includes the companies Sony, Matsushita, Hitachi and Philips. Blu-ray discs can store around 13 hours of standard video. Sony has been selling Blu-ray recorders in Japan since 2003, and Matsushita and Sharp have both (29) .... Blu-ray devices onto the market this year.

The battle between the two standards has heated up in recent months as the two camps fight to sign up hardware vendors and content producers, notably Hollywood studios, which have (30) .... the outcome of previous standards wars.

0	A argument	B contest	C opposition	D struggle
21	A incompatible	B inconsistent	C contradictory	D conflicting
22	A range	B dimension	C capacity	D extent
23	A advertise	B further	C push	D boost
24	A approving	B enabling	C equipping	D authorising
25	A advertised	B supported	C marketed	D encouraged
26	A specification	B precision	C illustration	D definition
27	A qualification	B limitation	C restriction	D modification
28	A board	B consortium	C jury	D committee
29	A founded	B established	C launched	D dispatched
30	A determined	B concluded	C solved	D resulted

PART FIVE

Questions 31 – 40

- Read the article below about a retailer.
- For each question **31 – 40**, write one word in CAPITAL LETTERS.
- There is an example at the beginning, **(0)**.

Littlewoods rethinks catalogue strategy

The retailer Littlewoods is reviewing the PR strategy across **(0)** *ITS* home-shopping brands. The retailer is looking to rejuvenate what it offers in **(31)** .... face of fierce competition from firms **(32)** .... as Next Directory, cable TV shopping and websites. PR work for brands including LX Direct is up for grabs, in addition **(33)** .... sub-brands under the Shop Direct umbrella, for example Kays Lifestyle, Abound and Additions Direct. 'We are looking at this **(34)** .... a brand-by-brand basis and won't necessarily hire [just] one agency,' said a Littlewoods spokesman, adding that the review had been motivated by 'standard business practice'. It **(35)** .... thought that around six agencies will take part **(36)** .... a pitch process for which firms have been asked to submit written proposals. Agencies including Brazen PR and Cohn & Wolfe currently promote brands within the Littlewoods empire. The spokesman declined to specify **(37)** .... their roles could be in a revamped agency line-up. Any agency appointed would report to individual brand directors for the brands up for grabs. Littlewoods, owned **(38)** .... the Barclay brothers, hit the headlines late last month, **(39)** .... it revealed that it was planning to close 126 of its loss-making Index catalogue-based shops. The decision followed nearly 20 years of losses at the chain. The Barclay brothers bought Littlewoods from the Moores family in 2002 **(40)** .... £759m.

PART SIX

Questions 41 – 52

- Read the text below about non-financial reporting.

- In most of the lines **41 – 52** there is one extra word. It is either grammatically incorrect or does not fit in with the meaning of the text. Some lines, however, are correct.

- If a line is correct, write CORRECT.

- If there is an extra word in the line, write **the extra word** in CAPITAL LETTERS.

- The exercise begins with two examples, **(0)** and **(00)**.

Ethical business?

0	*CORRECT*	Co-operative Financial Services (CFS) is a medium-size banking and
00	*AND*	insurance business and with its roots firmly in the north of England and the
41		19th century. But in one respect at very least it is a 21st century world leader.
42		In a ranking of firms' non-financial reports, CFS came out at top, ahead of
43		second-placed Novo Nordisk, a Danish drug company, and BP, the British oil
44		giant. The ranking, which published this week, has been prepared by the UN
45		Environment Programme, and SustainAbility, a consultancy, in the partnership
46		with the credit-rating agency Standard & Poor's. In their non-financial reports,
47		firms volunteer such an overview of their 'environmental and social impact'
48		during the previous year. Since the last such ranking, many more of firms
49		have chosen to produce non-financial reports. It is also been claimed their
50		quality has increased – as, less happily for the environment, has their own
51		length. What was, ten years ago, a voluntary practice is now becoming
52		mainstream – in Europe, at least. Only these two American firms are in the top 20, but several of Europe's biggest businesses are there.

WRITING TEST

PART ONE

- The chart below shows the cost of buying two computers in three different shops since the year 2000.

- Using the information from the chart, write a short **report** comparing the prices for the computers.

- **Write 100–120 words.**

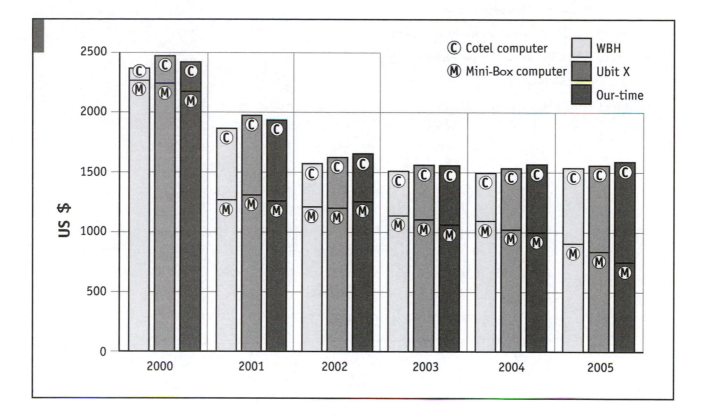

PART TWO

- Your company has decided to look into using a local venue for holding in-house training for company staff. Your boss has asked you to research and then recommend a suitable venue, for the HR Director to approve.

- Write your **proposal**, including the following:

  - a summary of the types of training your company runs

  - your criteria for selecting a venue

  - an evaluation of two or more local venues

  - a recommendation for a local venue.

- **Write 200–250 words.**

  Note that in the BEC exam, you will be offered a choice of three questions.

LISTENING

PART ONE (CD Track 20)

Questions 1 – 12

- You will hear part of a radio programme about a company called Target.

- As you listen, complete the notes for questions **1 – 12**, using up to **three** words or a number.

- You will hear the recording twice.

Company profile: Target

Target is a large American (1) ....

It may export its (2) ....

It has (3) .... shops throughout the US.

It is envied by its US (4) ....

Sales reached (5) .... 12 months ago.

Typical shoppers have a (6) .... of ca $50,000 p.a.

It has a wide (7) .... of products.

It (8) .... own-brand goods.

It runs very classy (9) ....

Recently it offered people on holiday (10) .... goods.

It has sold the Marshall Field's chain of (11) ....

It aims to carry on (12) ....

PART TWO (CD Track 21)

Questions 13 – 22

- You will hear five different people talking about training courses.

- For each extract there are two tasks. For Task One, choose the course described from the list **A – H**. For Task Two, choose the piece of advice given from the list **A – H**.

- You will hear the recording twice.

Task One – Courses

- For questions **13 – 17**, match the extracts with the courses, listed **A – H**.

- For each extract, choose the course described.

- Write one letter **(A – H)** next to the number of the extract.

13	A Managing your – and others' – time
14	B Negotiating effectively
15	C Finance for beginners
16	D Presenting yourself in business
17	E Cross-cultural awareness
	F Developing management skills
	G Become more assertive
	H Improve your IT skills

Task Two – Advice

- For questions **18 – 22**, match the extracts with the pieces of advice, listed **A – H**.

- For each extract, choose the piece of advice each speaker gives.

- Write one letter **(A – H)** next to the number of the extract.

18	A Be an active participant.
19	B Go with a colleague.
20	C Prepare thoroughly before you go.
21	D Record the session if possible.
22	E Talk to others that have taken part before.
	F Discuss the implications for your company.
	G Make notes on key points.
	H Look at the future benefits for your work.

PART THREE (CD Track 22)

Questions 23 – 30

- You will hear two colleagues speaking at a conference about teamwork.
- For each question **23 – 30**, mark one letter (**A**, **B** or **C**) for the correct answer.
- You will hear the recording twice.

23 What does Nigel say about teams?

    A Real teams work closely together towards the same aim.

    B There are more management teams than others in companies.

    C Most executive teams are structured in similar ways.

24 Sandra says that executive teams often

    A enjoy great camaraderie.

    B resemble political interest groups.

    C fail to carry out key tasks.

25 What does Sandra say about the team at Mix?

    A They fail to reach financial targets.

    B They do not work well as a group.

    C They make life difficult for other staff.

26 Which of the following does the Mix team do?

    A delegate effectively

    B regularly update other colleagues by email

    C come up with lots of new ideas

27 Nigel came to the conclusion that

    A management teams are often unsuccessful.

    B executives sometimes need a lot of team-building training.

    C there are frequent problems with international teams.

28 What kind of company often has ineffective teams?

    A multinational companies

    B businesses run by the founder

    C small, family-owned enterprises

29 Problems are at their worst when companies have

    A taken on more managers than they need.

    B reached a certain age and size.

    C become too big for their premises.

30 What often happens in companies?

    A Executives get moved from department to department.

    B External consultants run training sessions for executives.

    C Teamwork is talked about but rarely if ever happens.

SPEAKING TEST

PART ONE

Sample questions

What's your name?

Could you spell your name?

Where do you live?

Do you like your job/studies?

What do you do in your free time?

What do you like best about your job/studies?

What's the most difficult thing for you about your job/studies?

How do you get to work/college?

What do you like about the place where you live? Why?

PART TWO

A: Marketing: how to promote a new brand

C: Investment: how to invest successfully

B: Management: how to manage staff effectively

PART THREE

Speaking at a conference

Your company has been invited to speak at a conference in Singapore at the end of the year. The conference theme is saving energy. You have been asked to decide whether your company should attend the event.

Discuss and decide together:

- the reasons for and against your company participating

- who might speak at the event and what the topic of the speech might be.

Audioscripts

So, as I was just saying ... Unilever has long been plagued by comparisons. As an Anglo-Dutch **multinational** with two boards and two **stockmarket** quotations it is often compared with Royal Dutch/Shell. And, as a consumer-goods giant heavily into soaps and spreads, it invariably has to stand comparison with its American **rival** Procter & Gamble. So, with Royal Dutch/Shell having decided to abandon its dual structure, and Procter & Gamble last week acquiring Gillette ... for $54 billion, expectations have been rising that Unilever would follow suit.

The company's announcement ... during the presentation of its annual results on February the 10th, that Patrick Cescau is to become chief executive and that Antony Burgmans, the Dutch co-chairman, becomes non-executive chairman, seemed to be the start of the unification of the binational company.

But there is so far no sign of a **deal** that would help Unilever to catch up with the new Procter & Gamble/Gillette combination. Colgate-Palmolive, the American maker of toothpaste, and Reckitt Benckiser, a European household-products company, are possible **takeover targets**. But Reckitt, for one, would be expensive. On February the 9th it announced an increase in its pre-tax profits to £770m ($1.4 billion) from £660m in 2003. Also Unilever's **debts** are high: at the end of December net debt stood at nearly £9 billion – $15 billion.

The company needs to sort out its own problems before it takes on the complex **integration** of another business. Last year sales were down by 6% and operating profits slipped by 9%. In September 2004 came the group's first ever warning that it would not deliver a promised increase in profits. That led it this week to scale back the performance targets it had set itself for the next five years.

Let's now look at some of the difficulties the company is having – Unilever's main problems are seen by many to be too little advertising; unrealistic performance targets; some unattractive products; and a lack of innovation. The firm spends 14.5% of its revenues on advertising, which is more than the 12% spent by Nestlé, the world's biggest food firm, but far less than the 20% that P&G splashes out on promoting its products. The problem also lies in the way that the company spends its advertising **budget**. It made a mistake in sacrificing longer-term advertising on television and other media for short-term promotions in an effort to stem its loss of **market share**. Other difficulties seem to ...

J: Jim Meister speaking.

M: Hello Jim, it's Meeli here from the PR department.

J: Hi. How can I help you?

M: I need to get out a press release soon about your office workstation project and wondered if you could check I've got my facts right.

J: Sure. What do you need to know?

M: Well, I've written that office staff will be able to control their workstation 'from the touch of a button' ... I mean when they enter the building ... and swipe their card, the lights in their office will go on, their computer will start up and colleagues will get an email so they know the person's on their way to the office – all helping to save staff time and increase productivity.

J: Not quite. We've got rid of the email bit. Trials of the prototype indicate that people feel they're being spied on – you know, all their comings and goings noticed by colleagues and bosses!

M: Oh, OK. Thanks, so the new workstation's still going to be launched in June next year, I believe?

J: No.

M: Oh, so what is the schedule for the project?

J: Er ... well, we're looking at November now as a possible launch date.

M: Oh, I see ... and what are the key dates and stages before then?

J: I can't remember off the top of my head, but I can send it all to you though if you like, along with possible dates for a press shoot.

M: Thanks.

J: So, when do I need to get the information to you?

M: Monday would be great as I need to send it out the following day. Er, does that sound reasonable to you?

J: Fine. I'll speak to ...

Unit 3 Teamworking page 12

Listening 1 (Track 4)

B: So, Gina, how are things going?

G: Not too good actually, Bill.

B: Oh dear. Tell me more.

G: Well, we wanted to book the Pesta Hotel for the conference ...

B: Go on, I'm listening.

G: Well, the venue's free every weekend in June except for the 17th – which is when we need it.

B: Don't panic. Let's look at ways of getting round this problem. How about holding the conference on the 10th of June?

G: That's a great idea, but it's so soon – and there's so much to organise.

B: If anyone can do it, you can. And, of course, all the team will be here to help you.

G: Well, OK. I'll get onto the hotel straight away.

Listening 2 (Track 5)

F: Good evening everyone, and thank you for coming to this Baxby's bi-annual business forum. I'm delighted to introduce our main speaker this evening, Professor Peter O'Driscoll, from Kenilworth University. Professor O'Driscoll is an expert in the study of teams within business and he's going to talk to us tonight about the changing views of what makes effective teams. Over to you.

P: Thank you. Well, let's get started. As many of you will know, Professor Belbin's categorisation of team roles is still widely used. But the way companies view teams is beginning to shift. Professor Belbin viewed the team as a whole made up of individuals, where the success of the team relies on the individual elements performing their roles.

Belbin's approach is valid because it enables people to understand themselves and others as team members. It increases the team's overall knowledge of how the team is constructed. But we would argue that effective teamworking emerges from a combination of individual and collective competencies, or abilities.

We are all aware of teams made up of highly competent individuals that fail to perform as a team. The task is to develop teams of competent individuals to perform collectively. So, our research looked at which collective competencies were required to bring about effective performance. We looked at a variety of teams, including project teams, work groups, football teams and jazz bands.

The study identified a number of differences between teams in terms of structure and stability. Business teams, for instance, are often *ad hoc* creations formed to address a short-term need, whereas an orchestra or a rugby team are more stable.

But even very short-lived teams share generic characteristics with stable ones. We looked at jazz musicians in jam sessions, where individuals come together for a one-off performance. Although bonding might not be expected to be significant in such transient teams, we found that the jazz musicians sought to establish a level of social integration.

We also developed a model for assessing the effectiveness of a team as a collective. The model takes into consideration the relationships between individuals – the links that hold the team together. It identifies 16 distinct competencies that are crucial to team effectiveness. These competencies are divided into four clusters, or groups, known as: enabling; resourcing; fusing and motivating. I'll explain these shortly ...

Using the new framework, it is possible to identify where a team might be strengthened. The best news for managers is that team spirit will not necessarily be improved by spending the night on the side of a mountain in Scotland. Moving on now to ...

Unit 4 Information page 16 (Track 6)

M: I've just been reading about a new research tool called Doris. You don't know who has designed it, do you?

F: Yes, it was GNN, in partnership with Information 360, the software producer.

M: I see. Doris is a strange name. What does it stand for?

F: Direct, online, read-time information system.

M: I can see why it's been shortened! So, how does the tool work?

F: Well, as far as I understand it, the tool will be installed onto the GNN's regional news delivery network.

M: What are the benefits to users?

F: Well, users will be able to download a toolbar that automates how information is delivered from various departments. It can also help users to search hard drives to locate documents.

M: Will there be many users?

F: Yes, about 90,000 people, I think.

Unit 5 Technology page 20 (Track 7)

1 A successful briefing requires preparation. For one thing, it is important to make sure that everyone who needs to be present has been asked to attend. Too often a briefing will go ahead with substitutes who just listen and report back.

2 If you were paying for a briefing – I mean, paying money rather than spending time – then I'm sure you'd really want to be clear about what you expected to get out of the event. One way to achieve clear outcomes is to make it obvious from the outset what the briefing aims to achieve.

3 It's important to find out if the briefings you give are actually working. Remember how much time and effort is involved – and make sure you're getting a return on this investment. You may want to use different sets of measures – for example, global criteria to apply to all briefings and specific areas for different types of briefings.

4 There are a number of potential errors that can be made during briefings – which is why it's essential that those giving briefings get regular help in developing their skills. Not clarifying tasks, making unrealistic demands, cutting people off when they're talking, and so on – these kinds of mistakes can easily be avoided, given the right kind of support.

5 Some people are good at briefing others. Some aren't. To brief others effectively it's important to be clear about what needs doing and by whom. Write down a list of tasks if you need to – and allocate each task to a member of staff present at the briefing.

Before ending the briefing, make sure everyone knows what they have to do.

Unit 6 Advertising page 24 (Track 8)

Listening 1 (Track 8)

F: Did you see the news last night about our new sweets ad, the one where the children are eating and talking at the same time?

M: No, why?

F: Well, you'll never believe it, but apparently everyone's been talking about the ad, people in the industry of course but consumers too – to cut a long story short, there have been hundreds and hundreds of complaints about it.

M: Really? I can't imagine why.

F: Well, while I was watching people were saying that the ad wasn't setting a good example to children – I mean, eating and talking at the same time. Just then, some parenting experts came on to be interviewed. They complained that the ad could actually be dangerous – small children could easily choke ...

M: That's not good for our reputation.

F: Of course not – in the end, our PR people had to get involved and say it was just meant as a joke ... Anyway, guess what happened next?

M: What? The PR director's been sacked?

F: No, but the ad's going to be banned!

M: Never! The management team aren't going to be very happy!

Listening 2 (Track 9)

Procter and Gamble, which helped to launch TV soap operas as a new way to market goods, is looking once again for novel ways to reach consumers. Three years ago it set up an operation called Tremor to recruit an army of several hundred thousand American teenagers. It uses these 'tremors' to discuss ideas about new products and to help spread marketing messages. In return, the teenagers get to hear about and use new things before many of their peers.

Getting trendsetters to buy (or be given) new products in order to influence a broader market is hardly a new idea. So-called 'early adopters' are a similar group, much sought-after by consumer electronics companies in order to give their new products a good start. But there is a wider group which marketers sometimes call 'prosumers', short for proactive consumers. Some people in the industry believe this group is the most powerful of all.

Euro RSCG, a big international agency, is completing a nine-country study of prosumers, which it says can represent 20% or so of any particular group. They can be found everywhere, are at the forefront of consumerism, and what they say to their friends and colleagues about brands and products tends to become mainstream six to 18 months later. They also vary by category. A coffee prosumer, for instance, will not necessarily be a prosumer of cars.

Such people often reject traditional ads and invariably use the internet to research what they are going to buy and how much they are going to pay for it. Half of prosumers distrust companies and products they cannot find on the internet. If they want to influence prosumers, companies have to be extremely open about providing information.

Suggested presentation (Track 10)
Good morning. Today I'd like to talk to you briefly about three groups of people that are important in the field of advertising: tremors, early adopters and prosumers. Let's start with tremors. These are usually teenagers that an advertising agency might use to discuss ideas about new products, as well as to spread their marketing messages. Early adopters are quite similar to tremors, and are used by consumer electronics companies to help get their new products off to a good start. Then there's prosumers, which stands for proactive consumers. Some people in the industry believe this group is the most powerful of all. They are said to represent about 20% of any particular group, and can be found everywhere. They are important because what they say to their friends and colleagues about different products often becomes mainstream six to 18 months later. They often research products and prices on the Internet before they decide what to buy. Now, let's look in more detail at ...

... Bernie Ebbers – the ex-boss who steered WorldCom through an $11 billion accounting fraud and into the bankruptcy courts – may not have been overly blessed with management foresight. Yet, in one crucial respect, Mr Ebbers, at least now, appears remarkably sensible – he refuses to use email. The ensuing lack of legal evidence, electronically tracing the fraud to the boss's door has slowed the work of government prosecutors, who until recently had secured guilty pleas only from four of his underlings. That changed this week with the capitulation of WorldCom's former finance chief, Scott Sullivan, who pleaded guilty to his role in the fraud. With Mr Sullivan now co-operating, Mr Ebbers was swiftly indicted. Developments at WorldCom mirror those at Enron, another famously fraudulent company, last month. There, a federal taskforce indicted Jeffery Skilling, the company's former chief executive, following a guilty plea and a co-operation agreement from Enron's ex-finance chief ...

Moving on now to InterContinental ... the company operates [1]_____ under its own name, and through such [2]_____ brands as Crowne Plaza and Holiday Inn. Once part of Six Continents, a British brewing, pub and hotel group, InterContinental was demerged in April 2003. Many of its 3,500-plus hotels were franchises, but those it owned were worth [3]_____ than $6 billion. Since the demerger it has sold 28 and put 13 others on the market. It then announced that 20 more are to go. The sales have been widespread: in America, Australia, Britain and even Vanuatu, a collection of islands in the south Pacific. The [4]_____ updated list of hotels being sold includes InterContinentals in Chicago and Miami.

But why sell now, when the trade is steadily getting back on its feet after three [5]_____ years? Well, because the bad times have taught hoteliers a lesson, except in the carefree late-1990s, their return on the billions tied up in bricks and mortar was lousy. It's [6]_____ more sensible to sell, and return some money to shareholders quickly. Then focus on running the hotels [7]_____ .

The thought is hardly [8]_____ . In 1993, for instance, [9]_____ Marriott International transferred all its hotels, along with much of its large debt, into a real-estate investment trust, which allows public-market investors to put their money in property. But the US company and the trust remain close. A [10]_____ example perhaps is Hilton Group, British-based owner of the brand outside North America. Since 2000 it has dramatically slimmed the $4 billion worth of hotels it used to own. It still owns about 70 of its over 400 hotels, but this is under close review.

Sale-and-leaseback is the [11]_____ exit route, and can [12]_____ attract financial institutions too that are eager for assets that let them diversify out of shares and bonds. Hilton in 2001 sold $440m worth of hotels to Royal Bank of Scotland and even more in 2002 to a rival Scottish bank; Royal Bank of Scotland had meanwhile put a [13]_____ $1.75 billion into a deal with [14]_____ Le Meridien. Now this might ...

Unit 9 Investment page 36 (Track 13)

S: On behalf of everyone here today at Wycroft Small Business Forum, I'd like to welcome Steve Walker from Aston Reinvestment Trust – Steve is going to talk to us today about the high and low points of his career.

SW: Hello.

S: So, perhaps you could tell us about ART.

SW: What ART does is provide loans at commercial rates to small businesses and social enterprises that have been unable to access finance from conventional sources, such as banks, despite the fact that they have viable business plans. The model we have put in place at ART, since launch in 1997, has been widely adopted by other finance institutions throughout the country.

S: What would you say has been your best decision in your career at ART so far?

SW: During my time at ART I would say that the best decision I have made is to ask for advice when I've needed it. We could not have put our model for lending in place without seeking support and information along the way. Running your own business can very often be a lonely experience. A lot of people worry that they may be looked upon as under-skilled if they ask for help. I was lucky because I had, and continue to have, directors who were willing to give their time to mentor me. So, if I have a problem, or am concerned about a particular course of action, I can ask them for guidance.

S: Can you offer businesses here today any other advice for becoming successful?

SW: Always be open to new ideas and don't be afraid to turn to someone outside of your field. It gives you a different viewpoint and lets you see the problem or situation from a different angle, which I have found often produces the best ideas and ultimately the best results.

S: What kind of companies does ART work with?

SW: ART deals with all kinds of enterprises, often with some form of problem within their operation – they may be under-capitalised, or be experiencing problems finding a place on the market for their product, and this is where ART is different from a bank.

S: Could you explain what those differences are?

SW: Well, a bank is there to lend money, to gain interest and make money for its shareholders. This is nothing like what we do – our remit is to encourage enterprise to flourish; alongside lending money, we want to help our borrowers succeed. We want to help them and we don't want our clients ever to be afraid to ask us for support. Hopefully we can point them in the right direction or provide help ourselves.

S: Have you made any bad decisions in your career?

SW: If I could go back and change any decision I've made to try and do it better, it would be one I made during the early stages of ART when I was trying to gain investment. I planned to have 50,000 flyers printed up to market the service and let people in the area know what ART was all about. My idea was to distribute 10,000 of them, and I thought, 'why don't we have them inserted into a magazine that goes out to all the wealthy homes within the area?' I didn't receive a single response from the effort, and I thought to myself 'how did we get that so wrong?' It comes back to listening to others, because I hadn't taken the correct advice on how to market our product. I had simply thought that it was a good idea and would work, and I was wrong.

S: What did you gain from this experience?

SW: This wasn't the correct way to advertise a completely new concept – but I did learn from the experience. I began to again ask for advice, look at other sources and see what other options were available. If I had sought advice from people more knowledgeable in this field than myself, I could have handled the situation a lot better and hopefully gained a greater response. So my worst decision also ties in with my best decision.

S: Where do you think other businesses sometimes go wrong?

SW: I think the worst thing you can do in business is to close yourself off to new ideas and interpretations of a problem or idea. If you're not afraid to ask for help, or support, or advice, and you take that advice on board, then you will always produce a result that is not only beneficial for the business, but also for yourself.

S: Thank you, Steve …

Unit 10 Energy page 40 (Track 14)

1 Right, let's look at what we've got so far – we're going to go for natural ventilation in the offices across our three sites rather than installing air conditioning, and we're also going to set up a car sharing scheme, where staff living in the same area travel to work together, rather than bringing their own cars … and we're going to do this by …

2 I'm going to begin by speaking briefly about petroleum itself, and then go on to look at the products we manufacture from it, such as chemicals and fertilisers. After that, I'll move on to discuss the problems of relying on petroleum – for example, as reserves become scarcer, the price of course becomes higher. Finally I'm going to highlight …

3 This piece of research was commissioned by the Institute for Alternative Energy and was published jointly with Montego University. The publication looks at a range of alternative energy sources and makes the case for reducing the consumption of, and dependency on, fossil fuels. These energies are evaluated against a set of criteria, including how affordable, reliable, accessible and sustainable they are …

4 In my opinion, the world's oil supply will run dangerously low by 2050 – that's why we need to be looking for alternative sources of energy now. I think people will be using a lot more wind and even wave power over the next 20 years – and who knows – perhaps also energy from animal waste, manure and that well, that's what …

5 When sulphuric acid arrives at the factory, it's taken off the lorries, checked and taken to a safe area of the site for mixing with other chemicals. The final product is put into bottles and then the bottles are stored for collection. The waste is put into barrels and these waste chemicals are collected for recycling.

Unit 11 Going public page 44 (Track 15)

(Part 1)

Let's start by looking at Google's first major development – online advertising based on an auction approach. Both Google and Yahoo! make most of their money from advertising. Auctioning keyword search-terms, which deliver sponsored links to advertisers' websites, has proved to be particularly lucrative. And advertisers like paid-search because, unlike TV, they only pay for results – to put it in simple terms, they are charged when someone clicks on one of their links.

Both Google and Yahoo!, along with search-site rivals **such as** Microsoft's MSN and Ask Jeeves, are developing much broader ranges of marketing services. Google, for instance, already provides a service called AdSense. It works rather like an advertising agency, automatically placing sponsored links and other ads on third-party websites. Google then splits the revenue with the owners of those websites, who can range from multinationals to individuals publishing blogs, **in other words**, online journals.

(Part 2)

This brings me to Google's new services, which extend AdSense in three ways. Instead of Google's software analysing third-party websites to determine from their content what relevant ads to place on them, advertisers will be able to select the specific sites where they want their ads to appear. This provides both more flexibility and control, says Patrick Keane, Google's head of sales strategy. Companies trying to raise awareness of a brand often want a high level of control over where their ads appear.

Now to the second innovation, which involves pricing. Potential internet advertisers must bid for their ad to appear on a 'cost-per-thousand' (known as CPM) basis. This is similar to TV commercials, where advertisers pay according to the number of people who are supposed to see the ad.

Let's move on to the third change – this is that Google will now offer animated ads. Google has long been extremely conservative about the use of advertising; it still plans to use only small, text-based ads on its own search sites. But many of its AdSense partners might well be tempted by the prospect of earning a share of revenue from display and animated ads too, especially as such ads are likely to be more appealing to some of the big-brand advertisers.

To sum up, there is a lot more growth to come as companies become more familiar with online advertising. **As this chart shows**, many big firms still allocate only 2–4% of their marketing budgets to the internet, although it represents about 15% of consumers' media consumption – a share that is growing. Many young people already spend more time online than they do watching TV.

If Google can prove that bidding for display ads works, then its rivals are bound to follow with similar services. This could shake the industry up even further. I'd like not to …

Unit 12   Competition page 48 (Track 16)

P: Today in the studio we have Rob Delaney, author of best-selling business book *Love your customer*. Rob's going to give us his views on the increasing importance of consumer power. Hello, Rob, and welcome to the studio.

R: Thanks, Pat.

P: So, Rob, we've heard a lot recently about consumer power. Why is this important?

R: Consumer power has profound implications for companies, because it is changing the way the world shops. Many firms already describe themselves as 'customer-driven' or 'consumer-centric'. Now – thanks to the internet – their claims will be tested as never before. Trading on shoppers' ignorance will no longer be possible: people will know – and soon tell others, even those without the internet – that prices in the next town are cheaper or that certain goods are inferior. The internet is working wonders in improving standards. Good and honest firms should benefit most.

P: I see. I suppose it is also intensifying competition.

R: Yes, today, window shopping takes place online. People can compare products, prices and reputations. They can read what companies say about products in far greater detail, but also how that compares with the opinions of others, and – most importantly of all – discover what previous buyers have to say. Newsgroups and websites constantly review products and services.

P: And this is changing the nature of consumer decisions.

R: That's right. Until recently, consumers usually learned about a product and made their choice at the same time. People would often visit a department store or dealership to wander around, seek out different products and seek advice from a salesman, look at his recommendations and then buy – or go to a competitor. Now, for many, each of these steps is separate. For instance, Ford is finding that eight out of ten of its customers have already used the internet to decide what car they want to buy – and what they are willing to pay – even before they arrive at a showroom, meaning that having posh showrooms to impress clients is of little importance.

P: I've heard that reaching these better-informed consumers with a marketing message is not easy, and not only because they are more sceptical.

R: Indeed, many people now spend as much time surfing the web as they do with television, magazines or newspapers, but despite the flood of product and price information suddenly available, consumers are unlikely ever to become wholly calculating. Tastes and fashion will differ. Brands are likely to remain popular. But brand loyalties are weakening. A slip or a delay can cost a firm dearly and hand the advantage to an opportunistic rival. This is how Apple's iPod snatched from Sony the market leadership in portable music devices.

P: I see, but many firms do not yet seem aware of the revolutionary implications of newly-empowered consumers.

R: Well, there are some businesses that have embraced the internet wholeheartedly, and been rewarded for it. Dell has by-passed retailers and used direct sales to become the world's top supplier of personal computers. The web is also transforming the travel business, giving consumers the power to book flights, hotels and cars directly. And it has allowed hundreds of thousands of small businesses, from mom-and-pop stores to traders of collectibles on eBay, to reach a global market.

P: Of course, and internet search firms such as Google, Yahoo! and MSN are now falling over each other to offer more localised services.

R: That's right. A service that consumers are sure to snap up. At a touch, consumers will be able to find a local store and then check the offers from nearby outlets even as they browse the aisles, or listen to a salesman ...

Unit 13 Banking page 52 (Track 17)

I have my doubts about the economics of the merger between UniCredit and HVB, and the challenge of dealing with two different languages and cultures. But two factors may act in its favour: HVB's urgent need to merge and Mr Profumo's track record in forging UniCredit out of several smaller Italian banks. There is also the advantage that no other merger spanning western and eastern Europe could expect such a good fit. The success of Bank Austria, which HVB bought in 2000, shows that cross-border mergers can indeed be successful.

What might the next such move be? In the past, Italy's central bank has frowned on foreign banks wanting to buy in Italy. Now that UniCredit has ventured abroad, the central bank might look more kindly on one of two other current bids, by the Netherlands' ABN Amro and Spain's Banco Bilbao Vizcaya Argentaria. The most pressure to merge, though, may be felt by Germany's Commerzbank. Commerzbank has spent the past year cutting its costs in investment banking and trying to go it alone as a middle-tier corporate and retail bank. But it will surely merge soon. Rumours have linked it with Deutsche and even with WestLB, a public-sector bank.

Deutsche's future is less easy to predict. Deutsche said no last year when offered the chance to take over Postbank, a retail bank owned by Deutsche Post. Now there are signs that Deutsche is aiming to expand at home and abroad. Deutsche is among those interested in Banca Comerciala Romana, Romania's biggest bank. Although Deutsche has operations in several central European countries, this would be its first big acquisition in the region.

Unit 14 Training page 56 (Track 18)

Ask a dozen business schools or management books what makes a good leader and you might well get 13 answers. They may agree, broadly, that a leader is able to motivate others, offer a plan that people agree to follow, inspire confidence and trust. But should a leader be tough or nurturing? Best in crises, or adept at avoiding them? Keeping an eye on detail, or allowing subordinates enough room to look after the small things?

The Centre for Creative Leadership, founded in 1970 in North Carolina, is as aware as anyone of the different theories about leadership. It has become one of the best-known business education providers not affiliated with a university; in the Financial Times' most recent listing of executive education providers around the world, the centre ranked in the top 20.

In 2002–03 some 20,000 students, three-quarters of them American and nearly one-quarter executives, took classes at the centre's five campuses, three in the United States, one in Brussels, and one in Singapore. The institute listed its 2002 revenues at nearly $58m.

The centre does such business mainly in the form of intensive, short programmes, many including one-on-one coaching sessions. Its clients include Citigroup, Nokia, Unilever, Xerox and several branches of the American military.

Before students even set foot on a campus, they take a series of questionnaires aimed at measuring their strengths and weaknesses. Other people close to the student fill them out too – the students hear how others see them, with coaches on hand to help interpret the results and make suggestions.

The centres take an individual approach to students' personal and professional development. It promotes access to coaches (for any amount of time from three days to a year) and runs simulations in which students can act out new roles. This offers the flexibility to try out the idea of being a leader in new contexts, which can be valuable as new business issues crop up. Also, the centre takes a broad and egalitarian approach: it sees all positions as having the potential for leadership. Unlike business schools, it tends not to show off about how its graduates go on to win big promotions. But such an approach ...

During the summer of 2004, Nokia, the world's largest maker of mobile phones, suddenly found itself on the ropes. Its market share in the first three months of the year had fallen to 28.9%, having hovered around 35% for years. The firm cut prices, but that was only a short-term fix; it then set about addressing the underlying causes. The unveiling of its latest batch of handsets provided new evidence that Nokia has changed its ways.

Nokia's woes had two main causes: uninspiring products which failed to address consumers' enthusiasm for 'clamshell' or 'flip-phone' camera-phones and highlighted Nokia's loss of leadership in design; and the company's reluctance to produce customised versions for mobile operators. Many operators have been turning to specialist 'original design manufacturers', or ODMs, mostly based in Taiwan, to supply custom handsets. These are often sold by operators under their own brands, to help differentiate themselves.

So the seven new handsets launched by Nokia a year later were telling. Four were 'slider' designs, in which the keypad can be hidden under the display, and two were clamshells. What's encouraging is to see Nokia dumping the 'not-invented-here' mentality and becoming a fast follower – this is the best new batch of handsets the firm has produced for four years.

This follows the unveiling in April of a new line of high-end handsets, the most advanced of which, the N91, includes iPod-style music playback from a tiny hard disk.

Meanwhile, Nokia has also changed its tune on customisation. As well as offering to modify the software on its phones to suit particular operators, it has started to offer custom handsets. The first is being made for China Mobile, with others to follow soon. And having traditionally been reluctant to outsource manufacturing, Nokia has started to use ODMs, as its rivals do, to plug any gaps in its product line. The firm has become more open-minded, more flexible.

Challenges remain, however. Having bounced back in the last three months of 2004, Nokia had a weaker first quarter this year, largely due to poor sales in the USA, where many network operators use CDMA technology rather than the GSM technology used in Europe. Nokia is said to have done a deal to buy advanced CDMA handsets from SK Teletech, a South Korean manufacturer, for resale under its own brand. This would beef up its range in the US, but would also be an admission that Nokia's own CDMA products are not up to scratch. Nokia says no such deal exists, but that may simply mean that no deal has been done yet.

Either way, it is clear that Nokia has changed its ways. The company has even licensed email and media-playback protocols from Microsoft, its arch-rival in the field of smartphones – something that would have been unthinkable a year ago. Nokia is so determined to stay on top, it would seem, that nothing is sacred.

BEC Higher practice test

Listening Test Part 1 (Track 20)

Call it cheap chic or class for the masses – whatever it is, the appeal of trendy goods at low prices has enabled the US retailer Target to grow rapidly in a part of the retail market where many feared to tread. Now Target is trying new ways to remain both upmarket and downmarket at the same time, just as some discuss it trying to take its business strategy overseas, perhaps with a foreign takeover.

With more than 1,200 stores in 47 states, Target has already expanded far from its roots. Its red and white logo of a bull's eye is increasingly in the sights of jealous competitors at home, who are curious to know how it has become the store of choice for a growing number of Americans, including many who could afford to shop elsewhere.

Target had sales of $41 billion this time last year, up from $32 billion in 2001, which makes it second only to Wal-Mart in America as a mass merchandiser, even though it is a quarter of Wal-Mart's size. The niche that Target has carved out for itself is as a classy low-cost chain.

Indeed, the typical Target shopper has a family income of over $50,000 a year, compared with that of about $30,000 a year for a typical Wal-Mart shopper.

Target offers a varied portfolio of items, from jeans and toys to sporting goods and consumer electronics. It does this by taking special lines, such as Isaac Mizrahi's women's clothing. It also commissions designers to produce own-brand items. These are sold along with staples such as tissues and cereal.

The mix includes more clothing than Wal-Mart. Target owns a company that specialises in sourcing clothing and developing products. Target then rolls out stylish advertising campaigns to promote the new clothing range. This summer, Target set up a temporary 'pop up' shop in swanky Bridgehampton, New York, to sell discount clothes to holidaymakers.

This year the company sold its Marshall Field's department stores and Mervyn's, a mid-market store chain, for over $4 billion. According to a spokesperson for the company, Target intends to keep on innovating. It'll certainly be interesting to see whether ...

Listening Test Part 2 (Track 21)

1   The training may look like a day out of the office, away from email and the phone, but it's actually an opportunity to significantly change ways that you work – like improving your listening skills. If you are going to make such changes, it's best to think about how and what you will change before you leave the office. Read around the subject, go with specific questions in mind, for example, about different approaches to closing that deal and getting the price you want, and give it the kind of attention you would expect if you were briefing staff on new ways of working.

2   Get the most out of the course by talking to people who have taken the course before – find out what the benefits were to them, what they feel they can now do better, and so on – do they now organise their points well? speak slowly and clearly? deal with questions from the audience effectively? It may be that having spoken to them, particularly about the difference they feel that it has made to them, that you decide not to go at all! If it doesn't look like it's going to help you at all, then you might as well spend the day in bed.

3   So, what room is there for improvement in your work? Look at the implications in terms of changing the way you organise your workload and deal with deadlines – both for yourself and your staff. Training is frequently evaluated on a single side of A4 – in reality, it should be evaluated in terms of the positive differences it will enable you to make in the coming days, weeks, months and years – in your case, this will particularly refer to your ability to prioritise tasks and allocate work most effectively.

4   Trainers will frequently allow you to ask questions during the session. There are often opportunities to quiz them about new software that's available, local service providers and so on. Take the time in coffee breaks and over lunch to ask more of them. They will have been to many companies facing the same technical challenges as you face and there will be answers to be had. Get an email address so that you can get input after the session, if possible.

5   After the training session, isolate the learning points and the possible outcomes for your organisation before you return to your desk. Don't just make it something you did for a day and then forgot all about. Then book a slot with your manager to talk through these outcomes. If you've got an overseas trip coming up or colleagues visiting from branches elsewhere in the world, see how you can take on board what you've learned. If you are going to make real and lasting attitude and behavioural changes within the organisation you will need the support of others.

Listening Test Part 3 (Track 22)

N: Good morning, and welcome. My name's Nigel Parsons, and this is my colleague, Sandra Woodall, and we've been asked to speak at the conference today about teams. So, let's get started.

The phrase 'top management teams' trips off the tongue so easily but do they really exist – as 'teams', I mean? When you look closely, executive groups hardly resemble any real team that might readily spring to mind. A wind octet, or a five-a-side soccer team: these are real teams by my definition – people cooperating fully in pursuit of a shared goal.

S: That's right, but executive groups are more akin to lobby groups, in which people bargain, form coalitions, compromise, and do deals to ensure that decisions are made in the manner they approve of. But it doesn't seem to matter much if there is an absence of locker-room camaraderie or intensive passing of the ball. Boards do OK – in fact, often quite a lot of essential business – without it.

But here's a strange thing. We've been doing some work recently with Mix Communications, a company where the leading group really is a team. This group is a bunch of quite brilliant guys who complement each others' skills and personalities remarkably well. This I know because I did some top team personality profiling with them. The trouble is that they're driving the next tier of their colleagues completely nuts.

N: They do indeed. They make lots of money and do a great job in supporting each other, just as a real team should. They are, though, forever having marvellous initiatives, setting hares running, and second-guessing their people. Emails rain down on the company's hapless executives day and night. And, as fast as the leaders empower, they disempower.

Once this paradox struck me – that you can actually have too much of a good thing when it comes to teamwork at the top – I realised that this situation is replicated in companies much more often than might be expected, and throughout the world. I mean, it's OK having executive teams, but they have to work well, which isn't always the case.

S: My impression is, teams that cause the kinds of problems I've been speaking about are a special feature of the small firm rather than large businesses.

N: And, in these organisations, the worst examples of tyranny by team are family firms.

S: That's right. Problems with teamwork are perhaps most dire though at what one could term late adolescence in the life history of a business. This is when the initial ethos is still creating a great dynamic but, as the business expands, it is beginning to be the unwitting cause of strains and cracks in the authority structure.

N: After a while, everyone gets so fed up – including the leading members – that professional managers are brought in from elsewhere. Everybody then breathes a collective sigh of relief as the firm slides into nice, solid, boring, corporate governance, where teamwork is a favourite phrase of both staff and management, but isn't actually something that takes place very often in the workplace.

Let's now …

Answer key

Unit 1   Alliances

Vocabulary (page 4)
Ex 1: 2 falter   3 clash   4 multinational   5 integration
6 prudent   7 acquisition   8 conglomerate
Ex 2: 2 on   3 in   4 over   5 on   6 up   7 out   8 down
9 out   10 down
Ex 3: 2 bid   3 partner/partnership   4 acquire
5 consolidation   6 achieve   7 merger   8 succeed

Reading (page 5)
2c   3a   4b   5d

Listening (page 6)
Ex 2: 2 consumer-goods   3 chief executive   4 chairman
5 takeover   6 15   7 6   8 performance   9 advertising
Ex 3: multinational, stockmarket, rival, deal, takeover
targets, debts, integration, budget, market share

Language check (page 6)
Ex 1: 2 CORRECT   3 CORRECT   4 didn't expect
5 we'll definitely have signed   6 CORRECT
7 did you hear   8 has been
Ex 2: (possible answers)   2 Here's my
3 offer electrical products and services   4 to hear more
5 When can we set up a   6 What did you think of
7 How can I help

Writing (page 7) Suggested answer
Dear Lesley
Thank you for your email of 25th June. I would very much
like to meet you. Perhaps we could look at how we might
share resources in our Eastern European centres.
Would next Tuesday (July 4th) at 10am suit you?
Best regards
Siobhan Philips

Unit 2   Projects

Vocabulary (page 8)
Ex 1: 2 resources   3 a problem   4 a solution
5 equipment   6 a plan
Ex 2: 2b   3a   4b   5a
Ex 3: 2 produce   3 supplier/supplies/supply
4 installation   5 review   6 allocate

Language check (page 9)
Ex 1: 2 (no article)   3 the   4 the   5 (no article)   6 The   7
(no article)   8 the   9 the   10 a   11 an   12 the   13 a
14 the   15 a   16 the   17 the   18 (no article)   19 a
20 (no article)   21 a   22 the   23 the
Ex 2: 2 When do I need to get the information to you?
3 Do you think July is feasible?
4 What will you need in the way of resources?
5 I think we should aim to complete the work by Tuesday.
6 Does that sound reasonable to you?
7 What exactly is involved?
8 How much are you budgeting for?

Listening (page 10)
Ex 1: 2 It will save staff time and increase productivity.
3 November
4 Tuesday
Ex 2: (See Language check 2) 1, 2, 6

Writing (page 10) Suggested answer
Dear Ms Watson
I am writing to apply for the position of project manager,
as advertised in the Telford Gazette on March 21st.
You will see from my attached CV that I have had over five
years' experience in project management here at Melbury's,
where I manage 25 staff and a budget of £2m. I recently
managed a complex IT software development project,
which involved dealing with numerous external partners,
sources of funding, and across several sites. This I
completed to time and within budget.
If you would like more information, please contact me on
024 9232 4411.
Yours sincerely
Geoff Mapole

Reading (page 11)
Ex 1: 2 system   3 plan   4 budget   5 negligence
6 programs   7 delays   8 schedule   9 launch
Ex 2: 2 true   3 true   4 true   5 false

Unit 3   Teamworking

Vocabulary (page 12)
Ex 1: 2 Plan   3 Establish   4 Create   5 Monitor   6 Keep
7 Ask   8 Ensure   9 Involve   10 Assign
Ex 2: 2a   3d   4d   5c   6c
Ex 3: morale, member, spirit, meeting, work, player, leader

Writing (page 13) Suggested answer (68 words)
Dear Simon
I saw your advert for sporting team-building events in the
Comet on 3rd July and am interested in finding out more
about these kinds of activities.
I would, therefore, be grateful if you could send me your
latest brochure and price list to the address below. I am
particularly interested in receiving information about
more adventurous activities such as bungee-jumping and
mountaineering.
Best regards
Russell Jakeman

Language check (page 14)
2 Team members must/should
3 You shouldn't
4 Mark can't have reminded
5 You should
6 I might have written up
7 Joe might be
8 You should
9 You shouldn't have got
10 He can't be

Reading (page 14)
Ex 1: 2 Professor Meredith Belbin
3 an opportunity to study teamwork in a controlled
environment using a computer-based business game
4 certain personality types were more successful than
others and nine roles are present in an ideal team
Ex 2: teamwork, team players, team activities, team
building, team spirit, team member, teamworker
Other team words could include: project, meeting, role,
leader, morale, task, goal

Listening 1 (page 15)
Ex 1: 2d 3f 4c 5e 6g 7i 8h 9j 10a
Ex 2: Let's look at ways of getting round this problem; That's a great idea; If anyone can do it, you can; all the team will be here to help you
Listening 2 (page 15)
2c 3c 4b 5a 6b

Unit 4 Information

Vocabulary (page 16)
Ex 1: 2a 3d 4b 5f 6e 7g 8c
Ex 2: 2a 3c 4a 5a 6c 7a 8c 9b 10b
Ex 3: 2 gather 3 hardware 4 intelligence 5 network
6 procedure 7 software 8 spreadsheet 9 surveillance
10 data

Language check (page 17)
Ex 1: 2 How about updating the website?
3 Don't you realise how busy I am?
4 Shall we have a meeting about the intranet?
5 Do you know who downloaded the files?
6 Do you have any idea how to install the system?
7 What would you do to get the information?
8 Why didn't you tell me about the new hardware?
Ex 2: b 1, 7 c 3, 8 d 5, 6
Ex 3: 2 won't it 3 will/won't you 4 did he 5 will
6 will they

Listening (page 18)
Ex 1: 2 does it stand for 3 does the tool work
4 are the benefits to users 5 Will there be
Ex 2: 2 tag 2, 3, 4, 5 open 6 closed

Writing (page 18) Suggested answer (123 words)
Email is almost universally used by businesses around the world, according to a survey carried out by Grant Thornton International. But there are wide variations between countries in both levels of usage and attitudes towards its usefulness.
Businesses in the Philippines spend the most time, an average of 2.1 hours a day, dealing with email, followed by Hong Kong, India and the United States at 2 hours. At the other extreme are Greece and Russia, where companies only use email for about 45 minutes a day. Firms in the Philippines, India and Mexico were most likely to report that use of the internet has increased their revenues. But a mere 13% of companies in France, the nation with the most sceptical attitude, agreed.

Reading (page 19)
2b 3b 4d

Unit 5 Technology

Vocabulary (page 20)
Ex 1: 2d 3c 4c 5a 6c 7b
Ex 2: 2b 3f 4h 5g 6c 7a 8e

Reading 1 (page 20)
Ex 1: 2 true 3 true 4 true 5 false
Ex 2: 2 that 3 which 4 who 5 which 6 which
7 which
Ex 3: 2 compatible 3 prototype 4 surf 5 components
6 devices 7 wireless 8 networks

Reading 2 (page 22)
1 the 2 of 3 and 4 CORRECT 5 in 6 that 7 it
8 CORRECT 9 be 10 seem 11 CORRECT

Writing (page 22) Suggested answer (70 words)
Re: new items for stock
Dear Daniel
I'd like to recommend that we add the XBOX360 to our stock list. It has similar features and functions to Sony's Playstation 3 – e.g. wireless internet and controllers and DVD player – but more memory. Although it's not as powerful as the playstation, it is slightly cheaper – and we'll be able to stock it shortly, as it'll be available by Christmas.
Best wishes
Silvia

Language check (page 23)
2a 3f 4e 5d 6c

Listening (page 23)
2E 3C 4F 5G

Unit 6 Advertising

Vocabulary (page 24)
Ex 1: 2h 3a 4f 5e 6d 7b 8g
Ex 2: 2 trade show 3 cost-effective 4 commercial
5 telemarketing 6 publicity 7 exhibition 8 glossy
9 promotion 10 stand 11 agency
Ex 3: 2 reduction 3 promotion 4 endorse 5 publicity
6 persuade 7 demonstration 8 cancel

Language check (page 25)
2 to present 3 working 4 publicise 5 to attend
6 setting 7 targeting 8 to liaise 9 cancelling

Listening 1 (page 25)
Ex 1: The first reason was that children were shown speaking with their mouths full of sweets. The second was because it could be dangerous – children could choke. The ad was banned.
Ex 2: c d e h

Reading (page 26)
Ex 1: Too many ads!
Ex 2: 2 slogans 3 consumers 4 commercial 5 brands
6 effectiveness 7 audiences 8 promoting 9 budget
10 media 11 campaign
Ex 3: b number of ad messages an average American receives daily
c number of ads providing a return on investment
d number of US households reached by TV networks
e number of brands examined in a report
f date when many companies decided to cut their ad budget

Listening 2 (page 27)
Ex 1: 1 an operation set up to recruit US teenagers
2 people who obtain products as soon as they become available
3 proactive customers who research products online
Ex 2: See suggested presentation in Audioscripts, page 82.

Writing (page 27) Suggested answer (78 words)
Dear Geoff
My name's Terri Baker and I work at Frankton's, an advertising agency based in London. I'm an advertising assistant, mainly helping out with the day-to-day administration, such as mailing our clients. I'm keen to move into a job that offers me a more varied role. I'm hoping that I'll find my ideal job in your Ads4you magazine – which is why I'd love to receive a free two-week subscription, as advertised in the Exton Gazette.
Regards
Terri

Unit 7   Law

Vocabulary (page 28)
Ex 1: 2a   3c   4c   5d   6d
Ex 2: 2 procedure/proceedings   3 to prosecute
4 withdrawal   5 accusation   6 to assess   7 permission
8 dismissal
Ex 3: 2 sustained   3 rules   4 leaked   5 resolve
Ex 4: 2c   3a   4b   5a   6c   7b   8b   9a

Language check (page 29)
2a   3e   4b   5d

Writing (page 30) Suggested answer (47 words)
Dear Kulvinder
Thank you for coming over to PC Publishing yesterday afternoon. I'm just writing to confirm that you will be offering us 8% discount on all future orders.
Please could you send us a quote for reprinting 2,000 copies of our annual report.
Regards
Susie Martins

Reading 1 (page 30)
Ex 1: IBM, Dell and HP are introducing recycling programmes; Apple is taking back old computers; Ebay is encouraging people to sell, donate or recycle their old machines
Ex 2: 2 are replaced   3 are recycled   4 accounts
5 have taken/are taking   6 came
7 has not yet been implemented   8 are currently trying
9 have had   10 has come

Listening (page 31)
Ex 1: 2 there's no electronic evidence as email wasn't used
3 Enron – it was a similar fraudulent activity, where the CEO was indicted after the finance chief pleaded guilty
Ex 2: 2 guilty   3 fraud   4 prosecutors   5 indict
6 bankruptcy

Reading 2 (page 31)
Ex 1: 2 lawyers   3 litigation   4 fraud   5 lawsuit   6 risks
7 debt   8 bribes
Ex 2: 2 true   3 false

Unit 8   Brands

Vocabulary (page 32)
Ex 1: identity, extension, awareness, image, manager
Ex 2: 2 prestige   3 reliability   4 exclusive   5 luxury
6 popularity   7 effective   8 elegant
Ex 3: 2b   3c   4d   5a   6d

Language check (page 33)
Ex 1: 2 for   3 of   4 in   5 up   6 towards   7 from
8 with
Ex 2: 2 I wanted to tell you before anyone else does.
3 Before we start I think you should know about the delay.
4 I like his idea but will it work?
5 This just needs a few minor changes.

Reading (page 34)
Ex 1: 2c   3a   4d   5b   6f
Ex 2: 2 making losses   3 is thought to be profitable
4 has parted company with Helmut Lang
5 thought to be up for sale
Ex 3: 2 quality   3 retailer   4 exclusive   5 streamlining

Listening (page 35)
Ex 1: b
Ex 2: 1 internationally   2 well-known   3 more   4 recently

5 grim   6 far   7 well   8 original   9 American-owned
10 better   11 obvious   12 easily   13 further   14 upmarket
Others: close, dramatically, large, carefree, widespread, steadily, financial, lousy, bad, rival, etc.

Writing (page 35) Suggested answer (62 words)
Dear Matti
I just wanted to ask if you've got time to give me a hand tomorrow morning with the Sensi Soap marketing campaign. I've got to send out a press release. Before I do, I think you should check it.
Perhaps we could meet up this afternoon and I can fill you in on what exactly needs doing.
Best wishes
Jan

Unit 9   Investment

Vocabulary (page 36)
Ex 1: 2e   3a   4g   5b   6d   7f
Ex 2: 2 entrepreneurial   3 bankruptcy   4 ethical
5 intuition   6 risky   7 analysis   8 diverse
Ex 3: 2 bilingual   3 under-spent   4 underestimated
5 prearranged   6 postdated   7 overvalued
Ex 4: greedy, focused, prudent, reckless, opinionated

Language check (page 37)
Ex 1: 2 Let's get Maxine to attend the conference.
3 It might be useful but only if we have time.
4 We really ought to do the review urgently.
5 The next step is to recruit new staff.
6 Meeting the deadline is absolutely imperative.
Ex 2: 2 On no account should you ...
3 Rarely have I ...
4 My boss has never ...
5 Not only did we exceed expectations ...
6 What our reinvestment trust provides is ...
7 Under no circumstances should companies ...

Reading (page 38)
1 any   2 even   3 not   4 is   5, 6, 7 CORRECT   8 be
9 extreme   10 which   11 such

Writing (page 38) Suggested answer (214 words**)**
Esta Bank
24 Blackhorse Road
Coventry
CV10 9JB

Press release
Esta Bank wins ethical award
For immediate release

Esta Bank's chairman, Remi Artand, will collect the prestigious 2005 Ethical Business Award at a ceremony at Coventry's City Hall on Friday, 2nd July.
On receiving the news that Esta Bank had beaten over 120 national and local organisations to win the award, Susan Lawrence, a spokesperson for the bank, said: 'This is great news – for the bank and for our customers. We've always believed that it's important to make investments that are socially responsible, promote sustainable development and don't harm the environment.
Clive Jason, a member of the judging panel, said: 'The standard of entries this year has been extremely high, but Esta Bank stood out – not just because of its excellent stance on ethical funds, but also because of the way it is promoting, through its seminars, understanding of the responsibility that organisations have towards current and future generations. It's not just about making profits.'
The awards ceremony will take place at City Hall from 3 to 5pm on 2nd July, and will be attended by over 500

representatives from UK businesses, as well as national and local media.

For more information about the ceremony and the award itself, contact Shelly Marsden, Press and Media office, tel: 02476 111331; email: smarsden@esta.co.uk

Listening (page 39)
Ex 1: 2b 3a 4a 5a 6c 7b 8a
Ex 2: 2 He is happy about his decision to ask others for help.
3 Steve regrets wasting time and money on a marketing leaflet.
4 He would advise other companies to be open to new ideas.

Unit 10 Energy

Vocabulary (page 40)
Ex 1: 2 catastrophic 3 shortage 4 consumption
5 extracting/extraction 6 dependent 7 sources
8 consequences 9 depleted 10 emissions
Ex 2: unacceptable; non-negotiable, non-renewable; illegitimate, illegal; impossible, impartial; invalid, insignificant; irregular, irrational

Language check (page 41)
Ex 1: 2 If you hadn't reminded me about the meeting, I wouldn't have gone.
3 CORRECT
4 If fluorescent bulbs were cheaper, I'm sure more people would use them.
5 What would you do if there wasn't such a good bus service?
6 CORRECT
7 If someone's already bought me a ticket, then of course I'll go to the show.
8 CORRECT
Ex 2: (Suggested answers)
2B ... be better!
3A Are you/we still on ...
4A Any idea what ...
5B ... comes to the worst
6A What seems to be holding ...

Listening (page 42)
Ex 1: 2d 3g 4f 5c
Ex 2: 2 affordable 3 alternative 4 ventilation 5 reliable
6 waste 7 accessible 8 dependency

Writing (page 42) Suggested answer (236 words)
Dear Sir/Madam
I am writing with regard to your energy-saving competition to tell you why I think Thassos Chemicals should win the $5,000 prize.
Over the last decade our company has introduced numerous activities to save energy. For example:
• We encourage all staff to use public transport instead of using their cars – to do this, we offer a subsidised bus pass to all employees and their families.
• We have produced a series of posters, which are displayed throughout the plant, illustrating the small ways in which staff can make a difference (e.g. turning off their office lights at night, not leaving their computers/printers on standby but turning them off at the mains).
The $5,000 would be spent on changing all the bulbs in the offices to low-energy bulbs, which may cost three times the price of standard bulbs, but not only last ten times longer, but save up to 40% in terms of energy. The company would require 300 of these bulbs, costing just under $3,000 in total. With the remaining $2,000 we would purchase a

number of dedicated recycling containers for plastic bottles, glass bottles and paper. A local charity would collect and empty these containers on a regular basis and would retain profits from selling the waste products on to large recycling plants – we would thereby be recycling our waste and contributing to a local charity's fundraising efforts.
Yours sincerely
Matti Beck

Reading (page 43)
Ex 1: 2 to 3 What 4 but 5 up 6 than 7 to 8 for
9 more 10 on 11 which 12 the 13 only
Ex 2: 2 its energy efficiency
3 in the US buildings account for 65% of energy consumption, 30% of greenhouse gas emissions and 36% of total energy use
4 aims to change the way buildings are designed, built and run
5 reduce energy consumption, environmental impact, running costs, legal liability, improve work environment, employees' health, productivity, property values and rental returns

Unit 11 Going public

Vocabulary (page 44)
Ex 1: 2a 3d 4c 5b 6d 7a 8c 9d 10d 11a
Ex 2: 2d 3a 4f 5b 6e
Ex 3: 2 underwrite 3 debt 4 disclose 5 commission
6 discount
Ex 4: 2b 3a 4e 5c 6g 7f 8h
Ex 5: 2 with 3 for 4 to 5 on 6 on 7 at 8 into

Language check (page 45)
2 is going 3 file 4 may take on 5 hear 6 is managing
7 is going to start 8 won't be buying 9 will receive
10 are going to invite

Listening (page 46)
Ex 1: 2 It auctions search-terms that offer sponsored links to advertisers' websites – they pay only if someone clicks on a link.
3 It puts sponsored links and ads on third party websites – similar to an advertising agency.

Writing (page 46) Suggested answer (76 words)
eBay became a public company in 1998. The company's share price rose quickly, reaching $25 in 1999 and $30 the following year. However, over the next 12 months the share price fluctuated, and by early 2001 it stood at under $10. Over the following three years, the share price picked up again, climbing steadily to reach a peak of over $55 at the end of 2004 before falling sharply. The company's share price has since recovered.

Reading (page 47)
2g 3d 4b 5 a 6f 7e

Unit 12 Competition

Vocabulary (page 48)
Ex 1: 2c 3a 4b 5d 6g 7h 8e
Ex 2: 2 aside 3 about 4 have 5 on 6 to 7 Whether
8 in
Ex 3: 2b 3a 4d 5d 6b 7a 8c 9d 10c

Language check (page 49)
Ex 1: 2 While   3 once   4 the   5 finished   6 ago
7 as soon as   8 than   9 without   10 whenever   11 set
12 what
Ex 2: 2 It's unique because the company grew up in one place; the managers and their suppliers see each other every day, making it a kind of hothouse culture.
3 He left Ford in frustration and thought Toyota might handle customer relations better.
4 Everyone at Toyota works for the customer.
5 Their relentless pursuit of excellence: when they hit one target, they set themselves another higher one.

Listening (page 50)
Ex 1: 2 people can compare products, prices, reviews, etc. online
3 rather than going to a store to look for a product and then deciding whether to buy it, people are more likely to find out about a product on the internet before going to the store
4 some, such as Dell, are using a direct sales strategy to sell its products; others, such as Google and Yahoo!, are providing localised services
Ex 2: 2 true   3 true   4 false   5 false   6 true   7 false

Writing (page 50) Suggested answer (242 words)
This report sets out a series of proposals for ways in which ST Electro can attract new customers to its Monroe, Romley and Standford brands of electrical goods.
1 Reducing the cost of production
The unit cost of manufacturing our products is almost 15% higher than that of our main competitors. This cost is reflected in the higher sale price of our goods, especially the luxury brand Standford. In order to lower the cost of production, we could reduce the number of suppliers we deal with for core parts, thereby saving money through economies of scale. We could also investigate ways of making our distribution network more cost-effective.
2 Improving brand awareness
We need to make all our brands more attractive and well-known, in particular to customers in their late 20s or early 30s who have a large disposable income. Although market research has shown that some of our kitchen appliances do appeal to young professionals (mainly the Monroe range of kettles and toasters), the vast majority of our goods are unknown to this large potential market.
3 Positioning our Romley brand products
Instead of settling for being a niche player, selling hard-wearing kitchenware for the restaurant trade, we should look into contesting the mass market. With the increase in popularity of TV cookery shows, many more people of all ages are willing to pay a little bit extra for goods that will last – and ones which they see the real chefs on TV use.

Reading (page 50)
Ex 1: New best friends
Ex 2: 2 that Apple will switch to using Intel chips
3 Intel were better suited to Apple's plans; also IBM chips were not as advanced; supply delays from IBM
4 IBM: small impact – IBM has bigger contracts, e.g. for game consoles; Intel: small impact in terms of profits, but it will be good PR; Apple: risky – software will need changing and there may be some disruption for a while

Vocabulary (page 52)
Ex 1: central, commercial, corporate, investment, clearing, microcredit
Ex 2: 2e   3a   4b   5c   6f
Ex 3: 2f   3c   4a   5d   6e   7g
Ex 4: 2 lend   3 bank/banking   4 loan
5 implementation   6 investment, investor   7 payment
8 recover
Ex 5: a secure, pay off   b make, pull out of, agree
c lend, invest, deposit
Ex 6: a institution, corporation, agency, company
b merger, takeover, joint venture
c pension planning, taxation, portfolio management, corporate debt

Language check (page 54)
Ex 1: 2f   3a   4e   5b   6c
Ex 2: 2b   3a   4a   5b   6a

Writing (page 54) Suggested answer (103 words)
Dear Bruce
I met Mr Thaker, the manager at MTO Bank yesterday. It seems that they do offer higher rates of interest than Bordesley Bank on some of their business accounts – but these are mainly internet-based. Mr Thaker was keen to stress their flexibility about providing loans to local businesses, but I'm not sure this is a facility we'd need. They do offer a good investment banking service, which we may be interested in exploring in the future.
On the whole I'd recommend staying with Bordesley Bank. They understand our needs, and their standard accounts offer comparable rates to MTO.
Best wishes
Samantha

Reading (page 55)
2 which   3 been   4 by   5 each   6 at   7 when   8 up
9 the   10 by   11 for   12 be   13 because   14 in   15 who
16 where

Listening (page 55)
Ex 1: 2 dealing with two different languages and cultures
3 HVB urgently needs to merge; Mr Profumo has a good track record; the proposed merger is seen as being a good match.
4 Italy's central bank may be more positive about other bids to merge.
5 There may be more pressure on Commerzbank to merge; Deutsche Bank's future is hard to predict – it's aiming to expand in Germany and overseas.
Ex 2: need, fit, challenge

Vocabulary (page 56)
Ex 1: 2a 3b 4e 5f 6c
Ex 2: 2 participate   3 motivation   4 manipulation
5 budget   6 achievement   7 impact   8 customise
Ex 3: 2b 3c 4b 5a 6b 7d 8d

Language check (page 57)
Ex 1: 2 up   3 with   4 on   5 to   6 of   7 to   8 out   9 in
10 to/out
Ex 2: 2 Come on. You've got to do better than that!
3 Would you like to take full responsibility for this?
4 I'm going to let you handle this.
5 We're all in this together.
6 It's in everybody's interests to take on more staff.
7 I'm offering an additional commission to whoever strikes the deal.
8 This is the last chance to sort things out.
Ex 3: 2 because   3 despite/in spite of   4 In order to/To
5 as long as/if   6 As a result

Listening (page 58)
Ex 1: Centre: one of best known business-education providers, highly rated by Financial Times, 5 campuses world-wide
Programmes: intensive, short, 1–1 coaching
Pre-course tasks: questionnaires filled in by students and people who know them
Approaches: tailored to student, unlimited access to coaches, role-play situations, believes leaders can be found at all levels
Ex 2: 1 motivate   2 business education provider
3 graduate   4 intense   5 session   6 simulation   7 coach

Reading (page 59)
1 been   2 CORRECT   3 so   4 CORRECT   5 very
6 CORRECT   7 as   8 CORRECT   9 any   10 CORRECT
11 such

Writing (page 59) Suggested answer (180 words)
train4business
Cheltenham Square
Milton Keynes MK7 SRT

Press release
For immediate release
Linking cooking and training!

Train4business has launched an innovative new briefing skills course based on cooking – really!
Penny Smart, PR assistant, explains: 'We're offering managers the opportunity to leave their offices behind and come and take part in a one-day "hands-on" course that, as well as being fun, will develop their ability to brief people correctly and effectively.'
Participants are asked to bring along a favourite recipe and, within the small class (maximum of 6), explain to the others how to cook it.
Former student John Higgins says: 'It was a great experience – and made me realise just how important it is to give clear, concise and accurate briefings. If you're telling someone what to put in your dish and you forget any key ingredients or tell them to take it out of the oven too early it's all going to go horribly wrong. You've got to tell people everything they need to know at the right time.'
For more information, call Penny Smart on 01926 222 222.

Vocabulary (page 60)
Ex 1: Actions: re-organise, regulate, implement, legislate, advise, outsource, tax (verb), co-ordinate, plan (verb)
Business areas: IT, auditing, branding, plan (noun), bookkeeping, corporate development, tax (noun)
People and organisations: advisor, professional-service firm, customer, accountant, consultant, auditor, SEC, multinationals, lawyer, service provider
Ex 2: 2a 3b 4f 5d 6c 7h 8g 9i

Language check (page 61)
Ex 1: 2b 3a 4c 5d 6a 7a 8b
Ex 2: 2d 3g 4a 5c 6f 7e

Writing (page 61) Suggested answer (220 words)
Until recently a number of barriers have made it difficult for other companies to seriously compete with Dalyan Estate Agents – for instance, only nationally-registered companies have been able to operate in this area of business. Also, as the first agency in this sector, with over 20 years' experience and more than 20 branches throughout the region, we have been able to offer the most comprehensive advice and support in the property business.
However, times are changing, and, while we are still seen as the most respected company in our field and continue to offer a high-quality service to individuals and companies, we are finding it increasingly difficult to maintain a competitive advantage. Smaller companies have entered the industry, offering specialised services at more reasonable rates. In order to defend our existing market share – and to increase it – we need to target our resources more carefully.
I recommend closing our least profitable branches and refocusing our energies on our most successful and busiest area of business: helping companies relocate to this area. By offering specialised services to this growing niche market, we should be able to re-establish ourselves as market leaders. However, the future will hold new challenges for us, not least the cost of implementing new government regulations targeting estate agents – and of course the difficulty of retaining good staff.

Listening (page 62)
Ex 1: (Suggested answers)
Dealing with problems: new handsets, customised handsets, outsourcing, more flexible and open
Future challenges: poor US sales, using South Korean supplier, licensing agreements
Ex 2: 3, 8, 10

Reading (page 62)
Ex 1: 1 ... a problem (e.g. managing the day-to-day accounts)
2 A good consultancy agency can manage and advise (e.g. on investments).
3 It gives tailored, customer-focused advice to all types of companies.
Ex 2: piece = peace; expereience = experience; expertese = expertise; mange = manage; companys = company's; advice = advise; ultimatly = ultimately; comercial = commercial; succes = success; busness = business; profesional = professional
Ex 3: 2 management   3 recommendation   4 success
5 knowledge   6 consultants   7 investment   8 regulation
9 legislation
Ex 4: b1 c4 d4 e2 f1

BEC Higher practice test

Reading Test Part 1
1D 2B 3C 4A 5E 6B 7A 8C

Reading Test Part 2
9B 10D 11F 12A 13E 14G Distractor C

Reading Test Part 3
15A 16C 17B 18D 19D 20B

Reading Test Part 4
21A 22C 23D 24B 25B 26A 27D 28B
29C 30A

Reading Test Part 5
31 THE 32 SUCH 33 TO 34 ON 35 IS 36 IN
37 WHAT 38 BY 39 WHEN 40 FOR

Reading Test Part 6
41 VERY 42 AT 43 CORRECT 44 WHICH 45 THE
46 CORRECT 47 SUCH 48 OF 49 BEEN 50 OWN
51 CORRECT 52 THESE

Writing Test Part 1 Suggested answer (113 words)
At around $1,500, the Cotel Model XX50 is currently almost twice the price of the Mini-Box Computer, which costs around $800. However, this has not always been the case. Five years ago, the price of both models was comparable. However, in 2001 prices of the Mini-Box plummeted to $1,250, a price which Cotel has not been able to compete with.
The three stores – WBH, UbitX and Our-time – have priced the Cotel computer model similarly over the six-year period, with WBH offering the most competitive prices each year. Prices of the Mini-Box varied only slightly over the period at all three stores. However, Our-time has offered the Mini-Box at the cheapest rate since 2003.

Writing Test Part 2 Suggested answer (203 words)
This proposal takes a look at the possibility of using a local venue for all Bookley and Price's in-house training.
Bookley and Price currently offer a wide range of training opportunities to staff, for example:
- one-day business skills courses for 20–30 participants (presentations, meetings, etc.)
- half-day IT training sessions (Word, Excel, PowerPoint, etc.) for groups of 4–6
- one-to-one tailor-made programmes.
The company requires a centre, situated within a ten-minute drive of our Lakeside headquarters. It should, ideally, be reasonably priced, have different-sized meeting rooms and excellent IT facilities (including internet access). Staff should be friendly, professional and responsive to the company's needs.
Springfield Manor and Cotley Hotel are both located about five minutes' drive away. While Springfield has a higher level of IT internet support and a wider range of meeting areas, Cotley is part of a prestigious hotel chain and offers slightly more reasonable rates than Springfield. Their meeting rooms are comfortable and well-designed, although most are suitable for groups of up to 20.
I would propose using Springfield, in order to take advantage of the more flexible range of rooms and the specialist technical support, particularly as the number of IT courses the company runs seems likely to increase.

Listening Test Part 1
1 retailer 2 business strategy 3 1,200 4 competitors
5 $41 billion 6 family income 7 portfolio
8 commissions 9 advertising campaigns 10 discount
11 department stores 12 innovating

Listening Test Part 2
Task One: 13B 14D 15A 16H 17E
Task Two: 18C 19E 20H 21A 22F

Listening Test Part 3
23A 24B 25C 26C 27A 28C 29B 30C